T0323349

Moral Human Agency in Business

In recent years, corporate accounting scandals have received considerable media attention, raising concerns about unethical practice in the business world. Faced with a decline in society's trust in business, research into the ethics of organizations and their leaders is now of critical importance. In this timely book, Ericson focuses on the moral human agency involved in business by leading the reader through the full span of the activities involved in coffee production, from bean to cup. Illustrating the ethical implications and opportunities of producing Löfbergs coffee, Ericson highlights the importance of the morally imbued connections made between practitioners and other participants. These activities can contribute to a sustainable, profitable and competitive future whilst accounting for justice through a reciprocity of mutual benefit and respect, and meaning and passion. Promoting the reintroduction of ethics in strategy research, this book will be of great interest and use to strategy researchers, business leaders, and sustainability directors.

Mona Ericson is Professor of Strategy and Organization at Jönköping International Business School, and affiliated with CeFEO, Centre for Family Enterprise and Ownership. She has many years of experience from teaching courses in strategic change, organization, and advanced research methods in business administration and from involvement in academic managerial activities. Her research interests include process thinking in strategy and identity, and philosophy of science.

Moral Human Agency in Business

A Missing Dimension in Strategy as Practice

Mona Ericson

Jönköping International Business School

CAMBRIDGE
UNIVERSITY PRESS

University Printing House, Cambridge CB2 8BS, United Kingdom

One Liberty Plaza, 20th Floor, New York, NY 10006, USA

477 Williamstown Road, Port Melbourne, VIC 3207, Australia

314–321, 3rd Floor, Plot 3, Splendor Forum, Jasola District Centre,
New Delhi – 110025, India

79 Anson Road, #06–04/06, Singapore 079906

Cambridge University Press is part of the University of Cambridge.

It furthers the University's mission by disseminating knowledge in the pursuit of
education, learning, and research at the highest international levels of excellence.

www.cambridge.org
Information on this title: www.cambridge.org/9781108421881
DOI: 10.1017/9781108378420

First published 2018

Printed in the United Kingdom by Clays, St Ives plc

A catalogue record for this publication is available from the British Library.

Library of Congress Cataloging-in-Publication Data
Names: Ericson, Mona Margareta, 1948- author.
Title: Moral human agency in business : a missing dimension in strategy as
practice / Mona Margareta Ericson.
Description: 1 Edition. | New York : Cambridge University Press, 2018. |
Includes bibliographical references and index.
Identifiers: LCCN 2017035903 | ISBN 9781108421881 (hardback)
Subjects: LCSH: Business ethics. | Strategic planning.
Classification: LCC HF5387 .E69 2018 | DDC 658.4/08–dc23
LC record available at https://lccn.loc.gov/2017035903

ISBN 978-1-108-42188-1 Hardback

To my son, Rickard

Contents

Acknowledgements

There are many people who have contributed in different ways to this book being written and to whom I am greatly indebted. First, I would like to extend a big thanks to Kathrine Löfberg, owner and Chairman of the Löfbergs Board of Directors, and to Anders Löfberg, owner and former CEO and Chairman of the Löfbergs Board of Directors, for giving me the opportunity to generate empirical material about the exciting and dynamic Löfbergs world of practising they are entwined with.

Many thanks go also to Thomas Andersson, Lars Appelqvist, Charlotte Blomquist, Eva Eriksson, Helena Eriksson, Johan Eriksson, Björn Forsberg, Per Grahn, Marlene Högefjord, Åsa Lindqvist, Martin Löfberg, Anna Nordström, Björn Norén, Kent Pettersson, Göran Sonesson and Charlotta Stenson. In spite of time pressure and involvement in challenging work they have all welcomed me and contributed most valuable insights into moral practising.

Further, I am thankful to Pontus Boman, Cathrine Dehli, Tord Karlsson, Eva Kristensson, Filippa Löfgren Orebjörk, Gun Nyström, Moa Näsström and Elisabeth Ringdahl Wik, who as customers and consumers have provided very useful information about Löfbergs coffee.

I owe a special thank you to Professors Leif Melin and Mattias Nordqvist, from whom I received an invitation to become part of CeFEO, Centre for Family Enterprise and Ownership, at Jönköping International Business School. At CeFEO research seminars, my research has been presented and discussed. Many thanks to all my CeFEO colleagues for your support and valuable comments!

Finally, I would like to extend my sincere gratitude to Valerie Appleby, Editor, Cambridge University Press, for inspiring me in the preparation of my manuscript. I also greatly appreciate the three anonymous reviewers' encouraging comments on my book chapters.

1   Travelling a World of Strategy Practising

This book travels a world of strategy practising through the aroma and taste of 'Löfbergs coffee', whose vast varieties and subtle nuances are reflections of good things in life. Once known as the Wine of Arabia, coffee has become one of the world's most valuable trading commodities (Wild 2004). Prompted by the psychoactive substance caffeine, coffee is associated with enhanced cognition and related clarity of expressions, a beverage enjoyed by people throughout the world. By using Löfbergs coffee as a hub from and around which a study of strategy practising radiates and flows, we also realize that 'good' is an ethical aspect, pronounced through the practising of morality as will and values.

At present, from the deictic here and now (Herman 1995), will and values extend into a past and a future, promoting a temporal-relational understanding of moral human agency (Emirbayer and Mische 1998). In order to advance our understanding of strategy as practice we must direct attention to morality and examine how moral human agency unfolds in practising as a fluid and open-ended process (Tsoukas and Chia 2002) as it is constituted in activities with which practitioners entwine.

The aim of the book is to contribute an insightful and interesting supplement to existing strategy-as-practice research through offering a temporal-relational conceptualization of moral human agency in association with 'good' as will and values. The conceptualization develops via a rather detailed examination of the agency-focused parts of strategy-as-practice research, positioned in relation to business ethics research in integration with corporate social responsibility (CSR) and stakeholder research, and via an excursion into moral-philosophical works before it is furnished with contours in an empirical-theoretical discussion of practitioners' ongoing exercise of moral agency. Devoted to the pursuit of research that substantially integrates practising and morality in recognition of the practitioner's existential entwinement with a world of Löfbergs coffee, the book intends to open up a new perspective of strategy practice. Like a piece of music worth listening to with sequences of sounds, interconnected melodies and themes, it triggers the development of new insights and experience.

Against a Dark Background

Against a dark background of unethical conduct in the business world an urgent need is to enhance our focus on morality in research on strategy as practice. As business schools have been held partly culpable for the financial crisis in 2008, there has been a considerable rise in demand for courses and programmes that prepare students for futures as leaders capable of creating sustainable value in business and for the social good (Chan, Fung and Yau 2013). Yet, as Ghoshal (2005: 75) asserts, business schools 'do not need to create new courses; they need to simply stop teaching some old ones ... Our theories and ideas have done much to strengthen the management practices that we are all now so loudly condemning.' Prescriptions that flow from the *Homo economicus* models have socialized students into an ethics of limited accountability (Gintis and Khurana 2008); 'Economic Man' is cold and calculating and does not worry much about morality (Stout 2008).

In order to promote and inspire responsible management and education we need to encourage strategy-as-practice scholars to dedicate more interest to research on ethics in practising. Society's trust in business has been eroded by actions that make people wonder whether business leaders have lost their moral compass and are motivated only out of self-interest (Nohria 2013). 'Business can be pure hell, because it is relentless in the pursuit of its goals: goals that need to be aligned with those of the society to whom it is responsible and to whom it should have allegiance and to whom it should ultimately seek to be subservient', remark Svensson and Wood (2008: 306).

More than two decades ago, Lewis and Wärneryd (1994) gave plenty of examples of deceptive practices in branches of business and industry. Still today, whistleblowers reveal corruption, embezzlement and fraud, and, as a consequence, boards of directors, CEOs and other strategy practitioners are replaced. Corporate accounting scandals and related financial irregularities have received considerable media attention in recent years. Enron, World Com, Tyco International, Arthur Andersen and Skandia, for example, all claimed explicitly that they had a code of ethics and based their operations on ethical values but were not effective in communicating and living the code and the values (Svensson and Wood 2008). Willmott (2011: 90) refers to the spectacular rise and fall of Enron: 'Enron presented the appearance of a highly reputable company whose commitment to probity was broadcast by its values statement and detailed in its sixty-four-page code of ethics.' But we need also to observe that there was a business system, comprising bankers, regulators, politicians, accountants, lawyers and capital market intermediaries that validated Enron's business methods, as Willmott (2011) points out.

Numerous other examples exist of businesses that officially ensure that they maintain high ethical standards but in actuality fail to do so. Media also report on family-owned businesses that engage in unethical conduct. Even if a family-owned business, as opposed to a non-family-owned business, is expected to be particularly concerned about ethics (Adams, Taschian and Shore 1996), ethical lapses occur. Ethical lapses in business conduct could result from an excessive focus on short-term results at the expense of long-term financial health (Nevins, Bearden and Money 2007).

Strategy-as-practice research must be carved out in the nexus of practising and ethics with a focus on moral human agency. By pulling back the firm-level curtains, in brighter light we can identify how morality is expressed and practised.

Ethical and Moral Reflection Required

Largely unaddressed in strategy-as-practice studies are questions of morality and moral human agency. Reviews of practice-based research elicit that doing strategy means actively participating in micro-strategizing activities and interactions in relation to macro-level structures (e.g. Golsorkhi *et al.* 2015). Scholars view agency in relation to structure, defining agency as the human potentiality to participate in social systems or refuse to do so (Whittington 2015).Without a concern for morality, human agency is consolidated in a single individual and elaborated through processes of sensemaking, discourse and materiality (Golsorkhi *et al.* 2015).Generally, human agency is derived in an organizational context and ascribed to an individual practitioner whose actions are consequential for the organization's direction and survival (Jarzabkowski, Balogun and Seidl 2007), seemingly ignorant of morality. As Clegg, Kornberger and Rhodes (2007) point out, we need to develop theoretical tools for ethical analyses of what people actually do when they engage with ethics at work. As does Bauman (1993) they accentuate the practical aspect of ethics.

Ethical and moral reflection is required in practice-based strategy research, Balogun, Beech and Johnson (2015) emphasize. We cannot ignore that ethical and moral issues run through every aspect of organizational and managerial work (Watson 2006). The notions that people have an intrinsic propensity for acting on conceptions of morality and need to be affiliated with groups make room for *Homo moralis,* the moral human being (Skitka, Bauman and Mullen 2008). But we should not limit our focus to a single moral human agent since morality is expressed and effectuated in relation to the Other (Ricoeur 1992). As I have pointed out elsewhere (Ericson 2014), with reference to Cooper (2005), we must not lose sense of a human world constituted of dynamic and mutable relations. This requires considering how agency in association with morality unfolds in strategy practising, exercised (lived) in relation to the Other, between practitioners. Practitioners are 'always responding to and anticipating an "other"' (Cunliffe 2015: 442). Practitioners are beings-with-each-other (Raffnsøe, Møl Dalsgaard and Gudmand-Höyer 2014). In the social dimension that emerges of people in relations to others (Plessner Lyons 1983), morality is not reduced to a discrete moment of individual choice of actions (Luco 2014).

How to distinguish the meanings of the terms 'ethics' and 'morality' has been debated. As Ricoeur (2007: 45) admits, 'Etymology is no help in this regard, inasmuch as one of the terms comes from Latin, the other from Greek, and both refer in one way or another to the domain of moral behavior.' Ricoeur (1992: 170, emphasis in original) reserves ethics for 'the *aim* of an accomplished life and the term "morality" for the articulation of this aim.' The term 'ethical aim' is translated from French *la visée ethique* and does not strictly mean 'aim', however; it refers to an intention that we are not necessarily aware of, emphasizes Franck (2014). Ethics and morality concern how we relate to other human beings and not only what is right to do, Taylor (1989) adds. This prompts, in the passage from the ethical aim to morality, a dialogic structure that incorporates otherness (Ricoeur 1992).

Otherness is also implied in sustainability, an important aspect of ethics and morality (Jennings 2010; Van Horn 2015). It directs our attention to nature as an Other to which we relate. Sustainable practising has increased in importance to the survival, growth and profitability of a business, and to be sustained over time a business must take into account its ecological and societal impact. Sustainability encompasses values that range from the preservation of human health to the biosphere (Hirsch Hadorn *et al.* 2006). Thus it is important to introduce a nature–Other with respect to coffee as a 'component' of the biosphere.

Historically, there has been little focus on the sustainability aspect in connection to coffee. During the seventeenth and eighteenth centuries, the spread of coffee cultivation was largely the result of the expansion of European trade and colonialism with slaves playing an important part in the establishment of plantation economies and coffee companies. As Wild (2004: 121) notes: 'The white masters ruled the roost. The pattern was initiated by the Spanish, followed by the Portuguese in Brazil in the late sixteenth century, and later by the British and French in the West Indies, and perfected in the American colonies.' With recent proliferation of sustainability labels such as Fairtrade, Shade Grown, Bird Friendly and Organic coffee, the focus has shifted towards the coffee farmers and their living and farming conditions. In Sweden, sustainability-labelled coffee is strongly associated with Löfbergs. With reference to Löfbergs coffee we gain insights into how moral agency unfolds through a range of activities with which practitioners entwine.

'Löfbergs coffee' is a term used in association with the brand 'Löfbergs Lila' (Löfbergs Purple), but is not limited to the brand. It dissolves into a variety of strategy-oriented activities – from bean to cup. 'Löfberg' is also the name of a family who owns a group of companies, the Löfbergs Group,[1] envisioned as 'the most sustainable coffee group in Europe that with passion, strong brands and the best tasting coffee delivers increased value for our customers and owners' (*Annual Report* 2014/2015: 8). Anders Löfberg, owner, former CEO and Chairman of the Board of Directors (personal communication, November 4, 2015) summarizes: 'Löfbergs coffee does not only refer to a specific material content … it opens up to a number of activities and experiences, including the customer's and the consumer's experience of an ethically good product and a company that focuses on sustainability throughout the entire value chain: from bean to cup.'

A Beautiful Group Portrait

The human Other actualizes a moral agency that cannot be reduced to an individual as a detached subject. Nor can moral agency be sought in and determined solely by sustainability. Moral agency extends beyond issues of sustainability, constituting interactions and relationships among practitioners. However, the missing dimension in strategy-as-practice research, defined in terms of 'moral human agency in business', cannot be constructed directly. The portrayal of the sustainable coffee group in public websites, annual reports and other official documents cannot be ignored. It immediately attracts our attention in its beautifully described ethics interlinked with sustainability.

We are informed about a coffee group, consisting of the Swedish parent company AB Anders Löfberg with subsidiaries in Norway, Denmark, Finland, England, Estonia, Latvia and Lithuania, that produces

---

[1] More information about this group, its ownership and subsidiaries is provided in Chapter 4.

about 10.5 million cups of coffee per day and in dialogues with its stakeholders takes responsibility for people and environment, ensuring that profitability concerns go hand-in-hand with climate concerns. This group represents great keenness for and devotion to morally good practising, ingrained in the owner-family's responsibility for the coffee farmers, the employees, the customers and others and even the biosphere. Representing the third and fourth generations, the Löfberg family considers this responsibility to be a prerequisite for a long-term sustainable, profitable and competitive business.

Nevertheless, a group portrait that highlights ethics can create an illusion of a whole that operates in conformity with moral standards and rules. It is thus imperative to reach beyond an organization-level description, critically examining *how* practitioners articulate the ethical aim when engaging morality in practising. The Löfbergs Group, envisioned as the most sustainable coffee group in Europe, represents a beautiful portrait that calls for presentation. At the same time, this portrait mounts a springboard that provides impetus for centring the focus on practitioners' morality-imbued practising. The empirical-theoretical focus thus shifts away from a predefined group context towards a context that forms as practitioners and others entwine with a variety of activities. Being committed to a relational ontology and *geisting* means effectuating this 'from–towards' movement.

Committed to a Relational Ontology and *Geisting*

Ontologically, 'human science' derives from a translation of the German *Geisteswissenschaften*. As opposed to the English word 'mind', which has mainly cognitive connotations, the word *Geist* refers to moral and emotional atmospheres that may reign in a lived space (Van Manen 1990). *Geisting* closely relates to lived experience as used by Dilthey (1985) for an exploration of pre-reflective dimensions of human existence. The notion of lived experience implies an understanding that extends beyond the practitioner's subjective experiences, causal explanations and generalizations (Van Manen 1990). Informed by Heidegger's phenomenological thinking, lived experience suggests a movement through a world as 'a kind of mindless *dwelling* that precedes any subject/object and hence any reliance on mental content' (Chia and MacKay 2007: 230, emphasis in original). Also Gadamer (1989), a student of Heidegger, saw lived experience as an ongoing integrative life process through which the practitioner relates to the Other and a past. From Gadamer's philosophical-hermeneutical horizon, it is necessary to mark a distinction between experience as *Erlebnis* and *Erfahrung*. *Erlebnis* permits plurality, referring to *experiences* a subject has, whereas *Erfahrung* in its singularity overcomes subjectivity and is something a subject undergoes. Thus a world comes into being in lived *experience* (as used in the singular form). Time in terms of temporality, accordingly, conveys existential entwinement with the world.

A relational ontology with its strong connection to lived experience gives primacy to an interpretive study that provides dialogical openness to a Löfbergs world of practising. If we use variables to identify what things are, a category like dependency to represent possible relationships between variables and generalities such as classes (Helin *et al* 2014), we risk neglecting lived experience. Stefanovic (2000: 263) underlines, 'The selection and classification of indicators cannot proceed as if it were merely a technical matter of identifying a single set of "correct" variables.' Instead, we should refer questions of knowledge back to lived experience (Van Manen 1990), offering a temporal-relational conceptualization of moral human agency in recognition of a human's existential entwinement with the world (Sandberg and Dall'Alba 2009).

From a lived-experience perspective, inspired by Heideggerian phenomenology and Gadamerian philosophical hermeneutics, the practitioner existentially connects to a Löfbergs world of practising, entwined with strategy-oriented activities that constitute practising in association with morality. 'A single action at a point in time is not a practice; it is the passage of time that converts action into practice ... any attention to practice also demands an attention to history and, in particular, to time' (Ericson, Melin and Popp 2015: 516). 'Passage of time' is a linear sequence of activities but also implies non-linearity because of simultaneous and overlapping temporal orientations, unveiled in practising lived at present.

Method Accentuating Interpretation and Understanding

Implied in a relational ontology and adjacent lived-experience perspective is a qualitative method that accentuates interpretation and understanding and draws on empirical material generated via documents and dialogues with practitioners. There are no data 'out there' ready to be gathered; '*research is creation and construction*' (Grand, von Arx and Rüegg-Stürm 2015: 90, emphasis in original). Dialogues help the researcher to get at least some glimpses of an ongoing integrative life process in which the practitioner is absorbed. Unable to grasp the richness of lived experience fully, the researcher can only rely on the language used, that is, practitioners' orally uttered and written words. Research committed to a relational ontology and *geisting* interrelates a human being's life movement with language, promoting the idea that language has its 'true being only in dialogue, in *coming to an understanding*' (Gadamer 1989: 446, emphasis in original). Understanding, intertwined with interpretation, fundamentally connects with language.

Dialogue is a form of talk that can take us to whatever the practitioner finds it appropriate to talk about. It begins in an interrogative space that allows the researcher to cross over into the world of the Other (Risser 1981). Referring to Wittgenstein (1953) and Bakhtin (1984), this suggests, according to Shotter (2006), an understanding of how we relate to the other person and make otherness available to us in the activities occurring between us and the Other. It requires responding to the utterances of our dialogue partner, refraining from following a checklist questionnaire. A dialogue emphasizes *participation* and is a process of direct face-to-face encounter; in a dialogue two or more people are making something in common, not only conveying certain ideas or viewpoints but ready to go on to something different that takes shape in mutuality. But as people can be very polite to each other and avoid issues that lead to tensions and conflicts, topics that upset are likely not to be brought up, resulting in 'cozy adjustment', as Bohm (2004: 15) observes.

In order to maintain relational consistency in method it is crucial in the dialogue not to reduce the 'practitioner' to individuality, being aware that the practitioner through 'absorbed involvement in the world' (Chia and Holt 2006: 639) is always exposed to, affected by and vulnerable to the Other (Ricoeur 1992). A singular body 'is not individuality; it is, each time, the punctuality of a "with" that establishes a certain origin of meaning and connects it to an infinity of other possible origins' (Nancy 2000: 85). This sustains a relational reality where being-with constitutes an irreducible phenomenon, as Christians (2003) highlights. The interpersonal results from the actualization of reciprocity and a willingness to meet the Other openly in dialogue with no intention to dominate, as Roger observes in dialogue with Buber (Anderson and Cissna 1997).

Practitioner is not just something you are but something you are continuously in interaction with others. Practising presides over the practitioner but since practising is not equipped with a voice we must listen to the voice of the practitioner and pay careful attention to what is disclosed about what goes on between practitioners. When the focus pans out of an agent's physically discrete position we are able to gain insight into that which happens between agents, expressed in dialogues with me as a researcher. It is through my encounter with this agent that the potential for inquiring into and contributing to the advancement of an understanding of temporal-relational moral agency arises. I make myself a co-author, not as to existence, but as to moral agency in business, expressed and effectuated by the practitioners in reflection of their specific reality.

Generation of Empirical Material The generation of empirical material through face-to-face dialogues with practitioners associated with the Löfbergs Group, the Löfbergs-practitioners, started in October 2011 and a few dialogues were conducted during 2012. In this early phase of the study, the dialogues into which I entered with the practitioners mainly revolved around the practitioners' involvement in activities carried out in the chronology of time. Although my initial intention was to focus on strategic activities associated with development and growth, I soon realized that focus needed to be shifted to morality in association with 'good' as will and values. The practitioners often referred to a good will based on the five values of responsibility, commitment, long-term approach, entrepreneurship and professionalism, when talking about their involvement in strategically oriented activities – from bean to cup. A reorientation towards ethics and morality was apparently needed in my study.

In 2015, the generation of empirical material intensified through numerous dialogues with Löfbergs-practitioners holding positions as directors and managers as these play a key role in the development and maintenance of ethical standards and the practising of codes of conduct and moral values (Carroll 2000; Nohria 2013). Once again I met with owners, the present and former Chairman of the Board of Directors, the present and former CEO, the Chief Financial Officer (CFO) and the Human Resources Manager. In order to provide some variation in the empirical material, practitioners not designated a formal position as director or manager were invited and dialogues were carried out with people working as administrator, employee representative, production technician, process operator, receptionist and tour guide. The very first contact (in 2011) was with one owner, at that time the Marketing and Communications Director. I continuously communicated with her for advice on practitioners to meet as the study proceeded. The bean-to-cup chain constitutes activities that link together efforts made by other practitioners than those directly associated with the Löfbergs Group. Coffee farmers, representatives of development and certification projects, customers and consumers of Löfbergs coffee were also provided room for making their voices heard, some of which only echoed in written material. By participating in a guided tour through the production facilities there was also an opportunity for me to gain information about the machinery and equipment with which Löfbergs-practitioners interact.

The practising described is of strategic character. Strategy generally implies 'mobilizing resources in ways that strengthen the focal organization's command of its environment and/or weaken the position of competitors' (Alvesson and Willmott 1996: 129). In this book, the focus is on moral human agency as it unfolds in practising that constitutes strategic-oriented activities that practitioners entwine with when developing the coffee business over the long run. From-bean-to-cup activities orient towards a future characterized by sustainable and profitable growth that generates competitive advantages and is therefore considered to be constitutive of a practising that is strategic in nature. But it is important to note that an organization is not 'there' and that strategy cannot be unequivocally defined. We must critically reflect on how to use the term 'strategy'. Blom and Alvesson (2015: 423) 'sound a warning about the tendencies of overusing and inflating the signifier and discourse of strategy.' The current study refers to *strategic-oriented* activities, and the practitioners involved in these activities are not necessarily strategy practitioners or strategists. It is difficult to use the strategy label for all practitioners. In the following, the term 'practitioners' refer to Löfbergs-practitioners (including three owners) while coffee farmers, representatives of development and certification projects, customers and consumers are referred to as 'other people' or 'others' with whom the Löfbergs-practitioners interact.

The face-to-face dialogues with the Löfbergs-practitioners, ranging from approximately twenty to ninety minutes, took place at the headquarters and in the Löfbergs café Rosteriet, located in Karlstad, the largest city of the province of Värmland, Sweden. I live in Karlstad and the geographical closeness of the headquarters, production facilities and the café Rosteriet has been a great advantage. Most dialogues took place in the café, a location arranged by the practitioners. For each of us, the café appeared to provide a comfortable and enabling environment for a dialogue. The dialogues initially focused on the name 'Löfbergs', its connotations and meanings and what it is like to represent Löfbergs. Further, the talk revolved around the historical development and the practitioners' interactions with others, their current involvement in activities and challenges faced.

The practitioners made references to sustainability and good will in association with values, and they were then asked to describe will and values and explain how they are expressed through activities. Consistent with a relational ontology, the dialogues centred on morality as inherent in the practitioners' activities, rather than as something they related to as being external to them. They revealed how morality in relation to the idea of the good comes alive and what it means to practise the values of responsibility, commitment, long-term approach, entrepreneurship and professionalism. The dialogue ended with a focus on the practitioner's 'Löfbergs life' and what makes this life meaningful.

At visits to five other cafés in Karlstad I met with the café owners, a director and a guest. In a busy café there is not much time for a dialogue. Therefore the talk concentrated around the one question of why Löfbergs coffee is offered. Moreover, I paid a visit to three cafés *not* offering Löfbergs coffee, expecting to learn more about the advantages of actually offering the guest coffee with the label Löfberg but these expectations were not realized.

In total, thirty-three dialogues were conducted, five of them via email. The medium of email seemed more convenient to use when following up on the guided tour and for accessing some of the customers as the dialogues with them mainly concentrated on one question. In addition, empirical material was generated from annual reports, sustainability reports, and documents referring to policies, code of conduct, good will and values, coffee farmers and networks in which the Löfbergs Group participates.

All dialogues were conducted in Swedish. The face-to-face dialogues were tape-recorded and transcribed verbatim. The parts of the dialogues that focused on practising in association with morality were translated into English. This entails an interpretation and understanding that can be described in terms of highlighting (Gadamer 1989). The highlighting includes transcribed text that provides insights into morality primarily with regard to how morality in association with good as will and values is effectuated through strategic-oriented activities. 'Language is the medium in which substantive understanding and agreement can take place between two people', says Gadamer (1989: 384). One must then be cautious about the translation of the meaning, understood in one context, to another context. This requires an interpretation that bridges a gap between the original words and the reproduced words and awareness that the translation cannot remove the fundamental gap between two languages.

The translated text has been submitted to the practitioners involved in the study. They have all been given the opportunity to read and reflect on the parts referring to the dialogues. Over the course of two occasions all twenty-six dialogue partners have communicated their comments, requiring only a few changes in the text, and these changes have been confirmed by submitting the revised text to the practitioners requiring the changes. In this process, understanding and agreement have taken place between *interpreters* because we are not activated as the dialogue partners we previously were when speaking the same language.

The translation and highlighting involve interpretation that makes mutual understanding possible. The twenty-six dialogue partners have given me the permission to publish the material and openly acknowledge their participation in the study under their full names.

Cultivating Dialogical Openness

The Löfbergs coffee product is used as a hub from and around which the study radiates and flows. It is then not about a monological approach to Löfbergs coffee, outlined as a case in the traditional sense, closing in on a single firm or group of firms, family business and family. Instead, the current study can be conceived of as an 'open case'. As we go along, windows are opened, presenting us with opportunities to gain insight into moral human agency in business through a description of activities with which practitioners, not only those associated with a family-owned business called Löfbergs, engage but also coffee farmers, representatives of development and certification projects, customers and consumers. The use of a context defined by the Löfbergs Group as impetus for a move towards a context that emerges through activities people live neither requires concentrating on a family firm, nor on an identification of family members in relation to non-family members. The focus on morality among humans is not limited to what occurs within a family firm or between members belonging to one category rather than another. In family business research, family and business are often approached as two coevolving social systems and such an approach is presented as being 'truly realistic' for an understanding of the unique characteristics of a family business (Neubauer 2003: 269).[2] Family business is described as an open system and attention is paid to its sub-systems (Shepherd and Haynie, 2009). The owning family and its members are 'there', immediately recognized without considering how they *become* in relation to the Other. An autonomous positioning of family business or firm and member as entities excludes the notion of a being that appears to us as a becoming in relation to the Other. When breaking through the enclosure of the same in terms of organization and member we realize the importance of otherness (Ricoeur 1992). This incites a break with the functionalistic perspective that characterizes much family business research (Helin 2011). From a relational-ontological standpoint, a family is not an entity related to another entity, that of a business or a firm, but is

---

[2] A family business can be described as a business in which a family has a share of ownership and voting rights that allows substantial influence in terms of control and management of the business (Neubauer 2003).

constituted of spatially and temporally shifting relationships. In the words of Cooper (2005: 1708): 'Relationality invites us to see the world as the movement of relationships between things rather than the things themselves as static or quasi-static structures.'

Crucial for advancing our understanding of morality in association with strategy practising is staying in 'living motion, not so much in locomotive movement, as in a dynamic interactive, expressive-responsive relation with the others and otherness' as Shotter (2006: 594) expresses it. It is also about staying in motion with theory, continually interweaving theory with the empirical material. The research process promotes empirical-theoretical interrelatedness, combining interpretation, under-standing and application. A temporal-relational conceptualization of moral human agency is not entirely guided by theoretical premises but is constructed as the empirical-theoretical discussion proceeds through a process in which interpretation, understanding and application are unified. The original model for this we find in the ancient cosmology where the interpreter of the divine will is able to apply practically the words of the oracle, as Gadamer (1989) informs us. Interpretation and understanding of strategy-as-practice text and moral-philosophical text are applied to the present situation, defined by a missing dimension in strategy as practice, that of moral human agency in business. The texts are not only repeated but critically reflected on and dealt with for clearly illustrating why strategy-as-practice research is lacking an interest in morality, what morality is about and why it is important to add the dimension of moral human agency to strategy-as-practice research. Since moral human agency is not a static phenomenon but extends in time and space, texts provided by practice-based studies and moral-philosophical work are also linked to text that probes into temporal-relational agency.

The strong empirical orientation of the book too fosters the idea that we must intensify our contacts and interactions with practitioners for furthering our understanding of their reality. We need to strengthen our relationships with practitioners and move practice and theory closer together (Pettigrew, Woodman and Cameron 2001; Sandberg and Tsoukas 2011), taking into account that there are no 'pure' empirical data in terms of facts to detect 'out there' or original founding thoughts to build on (Alvesson and Kärreman 2007). It is thus about cultivating dialogical openness (Hjorth and Johannisson 2007) to empirical-theoretical becomings of moral human agency. With reference to Löfbergs coffee it is, in addition, possible to shine some light in the darkness of unethical action mass media often bombard us with.

To Follow

With reference to a rich corpus of strategy-as-practice research, Chapter 2 dedicates specific interest to how agency is approached. As pointed out, in the absence of a moral dimension, practice-based studies centre on agency in relation to structure, sensemaking, discourse and materiality. The chapter also emphasizes that we should not limit our focus to a single human agent, applying a two-category language of agency-structure. Morality is expressed and effectuated in relation to the Other. This necessitates a more elaborate theoretical treatment of strategy, agency and morality. Hence, attention is turned to moral-philosophical works that help further our interpretation and understanding of human agency in connection to morality. While reminding us that the Greek philosophical tradition and its inheritors exhibited strong interest in ethics and morality, Chapter 3 accentuates that strategy-as-practice research can benefit from addressing this interest. The chapter provides us with moral-philosophical perspectives and concepts that deepen our insights into morality and agency, and makes us aware of temporal relationality with reference to iterational, projective and practical-evaluative dimensions.

Chapter 4 directs attention to the Löfbergs Group, interwoven with theory presented in Chapter 2. The empirical material focused on this group raises theoretical concerns primarily regarding sustainability, corporate social responsibility (CSR) and stakeholders, which are aspects of morality Chapter 2 deals with to a certain extent. Theory of relevance for understanding the group-related work is also added as the discussion proceeds in Chapter 4. In closing, the chapter points to the need to move beyond a group-related moral agency for shedding light on moral agency as expressed and effectuated in activities with which Löfbergs-practitioners and others entwine. Against a dark background of unethical conduct in the business world we should not feel content with a research contribution that merely directs attention to the organizational level. A beautiful portrait of a group of companies can create an illusion of a group committed to high ethical standards. Thus, it is important to go beyond the group-level description for making the actual practising of morality more transparent in connection to temporal relationality, discussed in Chapter 3.

To be able to put forward convincing arguments for moving beyond a group-related description it is, however, necessary to include such a description. Indeed, through a focus on the Löfbergs Group we recognize the need for a move away from it. Chapter 4 provides impetus for enriching our understanding of strategy practising in connection to morality, instigating a move towards Chapter 5, which directs attention to the projective, practical-evaluative and iterational dimensions discussed in Chapter 3. Relational ontologically, moral human agency is an expression of *geisting*. Then we cannot present as the only truth that which the group context of Löfbergs coffee informs us in Chapter 4. We must be receptive to the human Other and a lived experience that goes beyond what can be verified. This is accentuated through the from-towards movement which implicates a transition from Chapter 4 to Chapter 5. Thus two empirical-oriented chapters are included in the book.

In Chapter 5, the longest chapter, dialogues with Löfbergs-practitioners reveal that morality interlinks with 'good' as will and values and that will and values extend into a past and a future, promoting a temporal-relational interpretation and understanding of moral human agency. The empirical-theoretical discussion refers to a value chain that comprises activities related to growing, transportation, processing, distribution and consumption of coffee. It also directs attention to a past strongly associated with a good will that is based on the values of responsibility, commitment, long-term approach, entrepreneurship and professionalism. 'Our good will' context emerges as Löfbergs-practitioners interact and effectuate these values. This particular context relates to a world of practising to which the practitioners belong as social-historical beings.

Chapter 6 is the final chapter, emphasizing the importance of adding a temporal-relational conceptualization of moral human agency to the study of strategy as practice. Advancing beyond a bifurcation of agency and structure, micro and macro, moral human agency unfolds in the projective, practical-evaluative and iterational dimensions. These dimensions expand our understanding of agency in recognition of a morality that does not merely propose a means–ends instrumental morality in the teleological sense and a moral obligation in the deontological sense. When moving away from the Löfbergs Group context towards 'our-good-will' context we realize that a value-based good will constitutes a morality that also gives primacy to justice as reciprocity for mutual benefit and respect and moral direction felt through meaning and passion. As pointed out, ethics and morality concern how we relate to the Other as human, past and nature.

2 Strategy-as-Practice Research without a Concern for Morality

Notably lacking in strategy-as-practice research are studies that direct attention to moral human agency. As this chapter initially acknowledges, discussions around morality are rather kept within the limits of business ethics, corporate social responsibility (CSR) and stakeholder research. Initiatives for cross-fertilization between this research and strategy-as-practice research are largely missing. While business ethics, CSR and stakeholder scholars dedicate much interest to the organizational level, strategy-as-practice scholars account for the individual level but leave out issues of ethical and moral relevance. The strategy practitioner performs agency by actively participating in micro-strategizing activities that can be linked to organizational outcomes and changes on the macro level. Micro and macro levels in reference to agency and structure are brought into a duality relationship with a focus on the entwinement of strategizing and organizational processes, and aspects of sensemaking, discourse and sociomaterial agencies are examined and moved to the fore. Studies provide insights into a rich variety of practices and make us acquainted with practitioners who deal with ambiguity and novelty, are involved in language games and power struggles, and enact their agency in response to and in communication with material, yet without a concern for morality.

The chapter posits that we should not limit our focus to business ethics, SCR and stakeholders with reference only to the organizational level. Nor should we restrict our interest to the individual level, applying the duality framework of agency and structure without recognizing temporal-relational variations in agency and structure. For the advancement of our understanding of strategy as practice it is important to give relief to human agency in its ethically oriented varying practicality. As opposed to the noun 'practice', the verb 'practising' is then preferred, suggesting an open and fluid process that constitutes in a variety of activities through which morality is articulated and actualized.

In closing, the chapter suggests extending the focus to moral human agency under the assumption that moral human agency is lived in relation to the Other. In this is implied a being-in-the-world view that holds the practitioner to be intrinsically entwined with the world. It is through lived experience, conceptualized as an ongoing integrative life process, the practitioner always relates to others and a cultural past.

Strategy and Ethics Relationships

Strategy and ethics once were closely interlinked in works of Barnard (1938), Andrew (1971), Arrow (1974), Simon (1947), and Schendel and Hofer (1979). They referred to ethical ideals in relation to business, moral responsibility of management and obligations a business has to society, as highlighted by Hosmer (1994) and Elms *et al.* (2010). Since the 1980s, the tendency in strategy research has been to give more weight to profit-based performance measures (Elms *et al.* 2010; Singer 1994). It is rather within the field of business ethics, with its long tradition of studies of business and society (Freeman 2000), that a positive relationship between social responsibility and business performance has been validated (Husted and Allen 2000).

Business ethics has been a discipline in its own right for more than thirty years (Svensson and Wood 2008), reflecting issues that are topical in the corporate world (Painter-Morland and ten Bos 2011). A central question is 'how a corporation can be managed with appropriate attention to ethics' (Goodpaster 1991: 52). 'Business ethics is concerned with how ethical values interfere with or unite with commercial values', adds Brytting (1994: 71). Informed by descriptive and prescriptive aspects of economic affairs with a concern for the well-being of an organization, business ethicists examine decision making and measure individual and situational variables (Donaldson and Dunfee 1994; Ford and Richardson 1994). Uniquely associated with individual decision making are variables resulting from, for instance, nationality, age, attitude, religion and employment. Situational variables represent the pressure and the influence that come from peer groups and top management in the form of rewards and sanctions. Further, code- and rule-based approaches are relied on for seeking rational solutions through guidance from external experts, and collective moral rules are elaborated for determining and normalizing responsible conduct (Loacker and Muhr 2009). A bounded moral rationality is expressed in a social contract that represents a shared understanding among practitioners about moral rules of relevance to their business (Donaldson and Dunfee 1994).

'When we talk about "business ethics", we are talking about the connection or the interface between the moral discourse – ethics – on the one hand, and that of the logic of action – "the logic of management"–on the other', Gustafsson (1991: 1) summarizes. Through the described interface the exit-voice phenomenon is made accessible. Dissatisfied employees combine multiple escape behaviours such as daydreaming, lateness and absenteeism from work (Keeley and Graham 1991). They may decide to exit the organization, whereas employees who voice their critical views to correct performance lapses stay (Hirschman 1970). In case of partial exit, the management is inclined to honour past ethical commitments, not considering it sensible to make further investments. Stone (1994: 34) likens partial exit to an unhappy marriage: 'A continued presence – as some married people know well – is likely to block opportunities for the other party to form substitute relations.'

Business ethicists also discuss how philosophical work can be applied to ethics and business (Gibson 2007; Hartman 2013; Husted and Allen 2000; Painter-Morland and ten Bos 2011). As Bowie (2000) argues, the theoretical potential for philosophy in the guise of normative ethics can be realized if normative analyses are integrated with analyses of business practices. In homogeneous societies it would be possible to line up normative claims before business operations, but in a globalized world where moral differences could run deep, there is no rock-bottom moral-philosophical knowledge to rest on for moral guidance, remarks Hartman (2000). The great challenge for business ethics in the twenty-first century is to advocate morality that takes account of globalization as a macro context. By examining citations from articles published in top business ethics journals over the period 2004–2008, Chan, Fung and Yau (2013) conclude that influential business ethics research mainly relates to organizational behaviour and organizational structure. Business ethics studies are more focused on the micro context than the macro context. With reference to ethics-based strategies, Husted and Allen (2000) point to opportunities to re-conceptualize a firm's role in society. In the micro context of ethics strategy, CSR speaks of a corporation's obligations in the environmental macro context, assumed to be society.

Over the past two decades an awareness of CSR, originally focused on the institutional level, has grown and a large heterogeneous body of CSR literature has evolved. 'The acronym "CSR" conventionally refers to corporate representatives' voluntary integration of social and environmental concerns into their business decisions', note ten Bos and Dunne (2011: 242). Based on an extensive review of the CSR literature, including 588 journal articles and 102 books and book chapters, Aguinis and Glavas (2012) reveal that this literature predominantly addresses the organizational level. CSR, widely regarded as a source of competitive advantage, promotes convergence between strategy and ethics primarily at the organizational level. Combined with stakeholder theory, a key CSR task of a corporation is to perform as a good servant of society through balancing the stakeholders' objectives and demands.

With Reference to Stakeholders and CSR

Combined with stakeholder theory, the study of CSR expresses a view of profit as 'merely the residual left after some value has already been allocated to/appropriated by employees, other suppliers, or stakeholders more generally' (Elms *et al.* 2010: 404). In the absence of a precise definition, CSR is used by some scholars as a source of competitive advantage and by others as a response to stakeholders' demands (Moon and Vogel 2013). At a rather general level, the European Commission (Press Release Database 2016: 1) defines CSR as 'the responsibility of enterprises for their impact on society.'

Stakeholder studies stress the relationship between corporate responsibility and stakeholder responsibility (e.g. Husted and Allen 2000, 2010; Jones, Felps and Bigley 2007; Mitchell, Agle and Wood 1997). 'Stakeholder', originally a play on the word 'stockholder' (Goodpaster 1991), includes categories of actors such as owners, employees, customers, suppliers, creditors, local communities and interest groups. In Freeman's (1984: 46) classic, firm-centric definition, a stakeholder is 'any group or individual who can affect or is affected by the achievement of the organization's objectives', and it is up to the manager, who bears a fiduciary relationship to the stakeholders, to keep the relationships among them in balance. The firm must be responsive to the stakeholders (Carroll 1991, 2000) and, at the same time, be aware that it can be put at risk when ceding its control of CSR to external stakeholders. Stakeholders cannot 'fully understand a corporation's capabilities, competitive positioning, or the tradeoffs it must make', comment Porter and Kramer (2006: 81).

Many dimensions of a corporation need to be taken into account when performing CSR. Donaldson and Preston (1995) refer to the descriptive, instrumental and normative dimensions. The descriptive dimension arises from the intrinsic value of a corporation. The instrumental dimension establishes a relationship between CSR and business performance. It accounts for the practice of stakeholder management and the achievement of goals while taking into consideration that trust, trustworthiness and cooperativeness can result in a significant competitive advantage, adds Jones (1995). The normative aspect concerns moral principles of the behaviour of the firm. As Bevan and Werhane (2011) point out, it is also important to explore dimensions associated with the scope and applicability of a stakeholder perspective that places the firm in the centre. Global companies frequently find themselves in complex networks of disparate interests, claims and goals among an array of individuals, groups and institutional actors. When operating in diverse cultures, being embedded in larger political, economic and legal systems, a firm-centric depiction of stakeholder relationships may prevent the firm from accounting for a multiplicity of perspectives of others (Bevan and Werhane 2011). In research that centres its focus on service business, a multidimensional perspective is applied, constituting economic, social and environmental (ecological) dimensions.

Service business scholars adopt stakeholder theory in combination with CSR when developing a model for values-based service quality (Enquist, Edvardsson and Sebathu 2008) and deconstructing the dualism of a shareholder strategy and a social-harmony strategy (Enquist, Johnsson and Skålén 2006). A shareholder strategy assumes that a company's social responsibility is to increase profits, whereas the social-harmony strategy stresses the importance of integrating ethics with business, establishing trust among the stakeholders. Studies demonstrate that strong corporate values give value-in-use to stakeholders (Edvardsson, Enquist and Hay 2006), provided there is a fit between internal and external perspectives and communication (Grönroos 2000). When embedded in a company's core managerial processes and business practices, CSR, as a part of the service logic, positively effects customer satisfaction, market value and profit. Driven by a social-harmony strategy and a responsive and proactive CSR adoption process, CSR can avoid value destroyers such as child labour and pollution, which will cause customer value to deteriorate. By providing a clear set of corporate values and integrating it into the corporate culture, management is able to influence the employees positively to perceive social responsibility as important and behave ethically (Vitell and Hidalgo 2006). Aristotelian virtue ethics and other research on happiness are also applied for providing advice on production and service management (Sison 2014).

A proactive CSR adoption process directs our attention to strategic CSR, acknowledging that responsive CSR is not enough. Strategic CSR requires leaders in both business and civil society to focus less on the friction between them and more on their interdependence, Porter and Kramer (2006) maintain. Interdependence accounts for inside-out and outside-in linkages. A company's value chain can be used for analyzing inside-out linkages, involving operational management for charting all social consequences for the activities that make up the chain. Outside-in linkages concern the company's competitive context where areas such as transportation infrastructure, regulations, access to research institutions and local availability of supporting industries are identified.

Apart from responsive and strategic CSR, the rich corpus of CSR research makes us acquainted with concepts such as corporate social performance and social responsiveness (Wood 1991, 2010), responsibility management (Waddock and Leigh 2006), corporate social strategy (Husted and Allen 2000), corporate citizenship (Hemphill 2004), and global citizenship (Logsdon and Wood 2005), all of which also urge a corporation to do good in interaction with stakeholders and for society at large. To this list can be added corporate ethical identity, which includes the communication of an organization's ethical attitude and beliefs, co-created with external stakeholders (Berrone, Surroca and Tribo 2007), and corporate heritage identity, which in combination with CSR accounts for an organization's core values and responsibility to the social and ecological environment (Balmer, Fukukawa and Gray 2007; Blombäck and Scandelius 2013). Also a new paradigm is launched for strategy in society, from a network view promoting mutual value creation for the focal firm and the stakeholders to increase benefits and reduce risks (Sachs and Rühli 2011). Moreover, scholars examine how stakeholder theory has influenced various fields, including strategic management, business ethics and CSR (Freeman et al. 2010) and discuss how continental philosophy can be used in connection with stakeholder theory, CSR and sustainability (Painter-Morland and ten Bos 2011).

CSR is a multidimensional concept that accounts for sustainability, invoking the so-called triple bottom line (Elkington 1998) of economic, social and environmental (or ecological) performance (Porter and Kramer 2006).[1] By taking this multidimensionality into consideration, Blombäck and Wigren (2008) discuss the difference between large firm CSR and small firm CSR. The CSR discourse tends to limit the analysis of stakeholders to a large firm context, but when incorporating the individual level it is clear that CSR applies to a small firm context as well. Regardless of firm size there are expectations of managers and the organization they represent to behave in an ethically responsible way. By including the individual level, Blombäck and Wigren-Kristoferson (2014: 308) further show 'how owner-managers accept responsibility for matters external to the firm and how they respond to expectations related to their various memberships through corporate local responsibility.' The authors clarify the connection between the individuals'

---

[1] Sustainability and sustainable development are further discussed in Chapter 4.

embeddedness in the local community and the firm's corporate community responsibility.

Although there are studies that incorporate the individual level, practitioners, their interactions and relations do not attract much attention among CSR and stakeholder theorists. It is rather within strategy-as-practice research that the individual practitioner is offered a front seat. With reference to agency and in connection to the situation in which agency is performed, the capacity of the individual to make a difference is of interest, yet without explicit concern for morality. Devoid of morality, the exercise of individual agency is largely a question of participation in strategizing activities and interactions on the micro level in recognition of structural conditions on the macro level, as noted next.

Practitioners Introduced

Reviews of strategy-as-practice studies (Golsorkhi *et al.* 2015; Jarzabkowski and Spee 2009; Vaara and Whittington 2012) demonstrate that agency is a question of how the individual practitioner acts. Practitioners, whose actions have consequential outcomes for the direction and survival of the organization, are introduced as strategists or strategy practitioners (Jarzabkowski, Balogun and Seidl, 2007) without explicit concern for how morality entwines with and unfolds in their actions. Researchers report on a wide range of internal and external practitioners, whose agency has 'pure' strategic implications. Apart from members of the upper-echelon teams of the organization (Brundin and Nordqvist 2008; Brundin and Liu 2015), studies consider accountants and middle managers as agents exercising strategic competence when involved in calculations and budget making (Fauré and Rouleau 2011). Strategic consultants, gurus and business school teachers figure as producers and consumers of strategic ideas (Whittington *et al.* 2003). Also appearing are the mayor, signifying a benevolent and visible leader of the company, the street fighter, acting as the heroic guy, and the insider-out (Beech and Johnson 2005). The insider-out describes a character, a member of an executive team resigning because of alterations to the company's strategy and composition of the board and the executive team. By acting as social craftspersons, artful interpreters and known strangers, practitioners introduce, promote and guide strategic planning and influence the strategic outcomes (Nordqvist and Melin 2008). The social craftsperson is able to blend and navigate between differences, aligning people. The artful interpreter shows sensitivity towards the need for localized adaptation, and the known stranger maintains a balance between closeness and distance to allow for objectivity in interactions among people involved in strategic planning. Agency 'is embodied, being part of who the practitioner is and how that individual is able to act, but is always connected to the situation and context in which agency is derived', Jarzabkowski, Balogun and Seidl (2007: 10) point out.

By interrelating the practitioner with praxis and practice, a conceptual framework is provided for studying how strategy is done (Whittington 2006) and it is also shown how this framework links to theory on resources and dynamic capabilities (Regnér 2008, 2015; Salvato 2003). Both the micro and the macro level are taken into consideration. A crucial issue is the relationship between institutionalized (routinized) practice and practitioners as institutionalized agents (Johnson, Melin and Whittington 2003; Johnson, Smith and Codling 2010).

The Duality of Agency and Structure

Lacking references to morality, doing strategy means that the practitioner exercises agency by actively participating in micro-strategizing activities that are linked to macro-level structures. Agency and structure constitute a duality. Praxis, operationalized at the micro and the macro level, links activities to socially, politically and economically embedded institutions. Practices are routinized behaviour, exposed through daily activities. Routine is defined as 'repetitive, recognizable patterns of interdependent actions, carried out by multiple actors' (Feldman and Pentland 2003: 95).

Organizational routines, manifested in a set of formal procedures, norms, rules, habits, heuristics or 'genes', consist of performative and ostensive aspects (Feldman 2015; Feldman and Pentland 2003; Salvato and Rerup 2011). The performative aspect includes individual agentic action, and the ostensive aspect refers to the abstract ideal form of the routine, embedded in procedural knowledge. As with Giddens (1979) and Bourdieu (1990), the duality of agency and structure implicates a mutual constitutive relationship between the performative and the ostensive, suggesting an intimate connection of the micro and the macro. The performative aspect is 'essential for the creation, maintenance, and modification of the ostensive aspect in much the same way that speaking creates, maintains, and alters a language', clarify Feldman and Pentland (2003: 107). Organizational routines are not individual routines but build on the subjective understandings of multiple participants who ensure that each action of performance is a collective performance and the ostensive aspect to provide a ready-made justification of action.

But when strategic actors begin to question the conformity, legitimacy and isomorphism that adhere to institutionalized routines, change in and even resistance to existing routines are instigated. This can be exemplified by a study that focuses on an executive management team involved in a transitional period of privatization in British Rail. Johnson, Smith and Codling (2010) describe a gradual move from central control of the rail system to greater local independence of decision making. Their study exhibits that habitual agency rooted in past behaviour was exposed to alternative institutional templates that were more attuned to market-based demands. It is then important to understand 'self-ordered criticality', that is, a tacit social accommodation of structure that influences the practitioner's scope of agency (Cambell-Hunt 2007). Large-scale evolution can lead to the extinction of rules and routines that once gave current managers their power. Although preconditioned by structure, practices can emerge over time through practitioners' improvization (Orlikowski 1996). Agency refers to the human potentiality to participate in multiple social systems, following one system and refusing another, Whittington (2015) points out.

Inspired by Giddens (1979) and Bhaskar (1989), Whittington (2015) accounts for agency and structure as mutually dependent. According to Giddens (1979), agency is a necessary feature of action, and action has reference to activity of the agent. Structure is understood as *structuration,* the properties of which are rules and resources. Structuration may imply an enhanced capacity of practitioners to act through the command and use of material resources such as capital and property, and through authoritative resources that promote power and discretion. From the viewpoint of Giddens (1979), resources are the media of power, assigned both a transformative and a dominating quality. The transformative quality refers to the agent's capability to intervene in the world and the dominating quality concerns the utilization of resources for sustaining power relations in a social system. In reference to Bhaskar (1989), representing the critical realism tradition, Whittington (2015: 152) points to the foundational role of structure for human agency, remarking that 'the most one can expect of agents is improvisatory skill within tight margins of discretion'.

Also Bourdieu (1990) is concerned with the dynamic relationship of agency and structure. To grasp the interplay between agency, occupied with subjectivism, and structure, granted objectivism, Bourdieu (1990) adds *habitus,* which constitutes practice and is oriented towards practical functioning. Structure governs practice through *habitus* but not in a strict deterministic sense. The relationship between agency and structure is presented as 'the dialectic of the *opus operatum* and the *modus operandi*; of the objectified products and the incorporated product of historical practice, of structures and *habitus*' (Bourdieu 1990: 52, emphasis in original).

Practices are thus continuously defined and redefined between the objectified and the objectifying intention.

Drawing on Bourdieu, Gomez (2015) investigates how local micro and field-level macro phenomena connect. She points to agents and their *habitus* with regard to the mental structures through which the agents deal with the social world as well as the positions the agents assume in a field. Bourdieu (1990: 53, emphasis in original) posits: 'The practical world that is constituted in the relationship with the *habitus*, acting as a system of cognitive and motivation structures, is a world of already realized ends – procedures to follow, paths to take.' Industries and competitive markets constitute fields within which agents try to preserve and increase the value of their capital. The distribution of financial, cultural, social, technological and organizational capital explains the positions of the agents and their capacity to act in a given field. Practice is grounded in individual experience and is influenced by the field, which in turn helps to structure the field. Practice is thus about 'the enactment of habitus, personal dispositions and beliefs that agents have developed through their trajectory in the field', conclude Gomez and Bouty (2011: 924). 'In a comparatively stable society, the fit between the agent and the structure is not caused by mutual adaptations in the present, but by their match created in the past (or, from the point of view of the present, pre-established)', Weik (2014: 107) comments.

As indicated, strategy-as-practice research contributes many valuable insights into agency and its duality relationship with structure but without a concern for morality. Illustrated in the following, strategy-as-practice studies also dedicate much interest to agency when centring on sensemaking, discourse and sociomateriality. In relation to these studies we too recognize that moral human agency is a missing dimension. Sensemaking studies invite interpreting and meaning making agents with little room for a moral agent. Discourse studies direct attention to spoken and written words and their significance for strategizing agents, largely disregarding ethical positioning in language. Although some of these studies attend to subjectivity, clarifying that the individual agent is not a separated self but performs agency in relation to the Other, there is no notion of how morality is expressed and activated in this relationship. With the inclusion of a sociomaterial aspect, scholars point to multiple non-human agencies without referring to morality.

A Focus on Sensemaking and Discourse Agency

Sensemaking in strategy-as-practice research largely represents the empirical phenomena of thinking and acting through which individuals and groups in organizations deal with ambiguity and novelty, summarize Cornelissen and Schildt (2015). Sensemaking is often appropriated as a broad umbrella term originating in Weick's (1979, 1995) idea of cognitive schemes and recursive interactions between actors and interpretations. With little concern for a sensemaking moral individual, agency is exposed by studies with a focus on the socially negotiated nature of sensemaking (Rouleau and Balogun 2011), the active use of frame-based meanings in organizations and industries (Cornelissen and Schildt 2015) and the temporal work that involves actors' negotiations and resolving of differences in interpretations of the past, present and future (Kaplan and Orlikowski 2013).

Sensemaking-focused studies account for agency with reference to ways in which individuals' responses shape aggregated responses at the organizational level (Stensaker and Falkenberg 2007). Further, they account for political contests (Kaplan 2008), the role of emotions (Liu and Maitlis 2014), materiality (Lê and Spee 2015), the function of meetings (Seidl and Guérard 2015) and how middle managers contribute to the re-creation of order and collective sense of shared meaning in and of strategic change (Rouleau, Balogun and Floyd 2015). From the perspective of Tsoukas (2015), it is crucial to distinguish between deliberate acting and non-deliberate acting. Non-deliberate acting is a form of practical coping, which teleological-affectively orients the agent's sensemaking, although not in regard to a teleological-ethical structure. The teleological-affective refers to an inherited background, formed out of habits and customs. Through a focus on sensemaking we also gain an understanding of how sense is given (Maitlis and Christianson 2014). Rouleau (2005) directs attention to how routines and conversations influence both sensemaking and sensegiving.

Following the linguistic turn in social science (Alvesson and Kärreman 2000; Vaara 2010) and a broader acceptance of social construction (Berger and Luckmann 1966; Gergen 1999), discourse has emerged as a rapidly growing topic in the study of organization and management (Philips and Oswick 2012) and strategy-as-practice (Golsorkhi et al. 2015). This turn, though largely amoral in character, has brought to our awareness an agency performed through words, building on the definition of discourse as 'a set of ideas and practices which condition our ways of relating to, and acting upon, particular phenomena' (Knights and Morgan 1991: 253). 'Words, in both their spoken and their materialized forms in text, are some of the most powerful resources for making and signifying an organization's strategy', Balogun et al. (2014: 175) purport. Agency is reflected in analyses of emotional dynamics (Brundin and Nordqvist 2008; Brundin and Liu 2015) and strategic conversation

(Liu and Maitlis 2014), talk-based interactive routines (Samra-Fredericks 2003, 2015) and rhetorical constructions of ambiguity (Sillince, Jarzabkowski and Shaw 2012).

We also get a grasp of the complexity of a word-related agency through studies that examine the multivocality of strategy text, and the communication and dissemination of text within and across the contextual phases of authoring, translation and interpretation (Aggerholm, Asmuß and Thomsen 2012), yet these studies too tend to leave out ethical and moral issues. On the basis of Fairclough's (1989) work, which accounts for the dialectic of discourse and social structure, it is argued that intertextuality and interdiscursivity form a network of meanings and a long chain of agentic discursive acts that cannot be separated from their social contexts (Vaara 2015). Further, studies look into how the textual version of a strategic plan becomes authoritative over time through iterative and recursive relationships of talk and text and convergence of meanings (Spee and Jarzabkowski 2011), and the strategic plan genre of communication (Cornut, Giroux and Langley 2012).

With reference to genre, Langley and Lusiani (2015) make us aware of a set of conventionalized discursive actions that attribute rigour to strategy language and, in addition, professionalism and legitimacy. A strategy language that builds on social conventions contributes a distinctive terminology in the sense that 'the production processes of strategies are institutionalized practices characterized by intertextual negotiations and reworkings of text' (Pälli, Vaara and Sorsa 2009: 3–4). When language is played as a game (Wittgenstein 1953) the players collectively agree on and adhere to a specific set of rules (Mantere 2015), which, however, do not include moral rules. Language games are both enabling and restructuring. Referring to the future of the city of Sidney, Kornberger and Clegg (2011: 55) observed 'how strategy as a language game enabled the articulation of culture as an asset for increasing tourist number and boosting the city's brand image.' The use of time had performative effects through the talk about the future.

Strategy texts legitimate certain ways of acting and delegitimize others and have political and ideological effects, Vaara, Sorsa and Pälli (2010) add. Hence, there could be variation in genre. Depending on audience, communication purpose and the development of techniques, different texts are produced (Langley and Lusiani 2015). When strategy discourse enrols in legitimizing actions of organizations across private and public spheres, disparate audiences may be targeted. Then policy making agents 'should be sensitive to the full repercussions of transferring practices from one sphere to another', Whittington *et al.* (2003: 404) emphasize.

Discourse practice could evolve into a struggle but whether such a struggle reflects ethics inscribed in policy making is not discussed.

Drawing on the critical discourse analysis tradition, influenced by Foucault (e.g. 1972, 1980), strategy-as-practice scholars exhibit agency as shaping and being shaped by political processes and power conditions yet without accounting for politically constructed ethics. A critical discourse analysis locates senior managers' talk and text in contexts at different levels (Clarke, Kwon and Wodak 2012) and reveals that middle managers are able to resist managerial hegemony by initiating a strategy discourse of their own (Laine and Vaara 2007). A study of a global telecommunication company discloses that the outside market discourse was reinforced as the inside professional discourse, associated with engineering expertise and technological success, was devalued, mainly as a result of the lack of clearly defined strategy objects (Hardy and Thomas 2014). Using the French term *savoir*, Allard-Poesi (2015) maintains that the extra-discursive formation of a strategy, governed by a set of power-knowledge statements, is dependent on material conditions not exclusively defined by what is said.

Through a focus on power and power relations, the Foucauldian tradition interrogates the hegemonic nature of discourse as well as the parochialism, which refers to the tendency among some discourse scholars to engage in a one-level type of analysis (Philips and Oswick 2012). A critical discourse analysis offers a multilevel approach that helps overcome the dichotomization of small d and big D. The small d constrains itself to fine-grained discursive work at the microlevel and the big D draws macro level pictures, Alvesson and Kärreman (2011) clarify.

Agency is closely linked to subjectivity. 'The discursive practice is productive of a sense of self, as well as associated beliefs about the location of power either as a possession of subjects (agency) or as an enabling and disabling condition of agency (structure)', Ezzamel and Willmott (2008: 195) posit. In accordance with Dameron and Torset (2014), the power aspect of strategy discourse explains how subjectivity is positioned and how identity and agency are protected and enhanced in relation to various types of tensions. A tension-based representation of strategizing gives subjectivity different labels. Dameron and Torset (2014) distinguish myticizing, concretizing and dialogizing subjectivities. The myticizing subjectivity is driven by intuition, the concretizing subjectivity masters analytic tools and gives tangible form to strategizing, and the dialogizing subjectivity depicts strategizing as a participatory and bargaining process. Efforts to mobilize discourses 'to discipline subjectivity are doomed to degrees of failure as they arbitrarily partition the world in ways that produce conditions of possibility of their breach', comment Ezzamel and Willmott (2008: 195). The efforts to mobilize discourses do not, however, include practices constituted in ethical activities. There is no self that in relation to the Other makes room for an ethical aim that can be translated to a sense of justice. As Cunliffe (2002: 131) insists, in language 'possibilities arise for relating with others in more reflexive, responsive, and ethical ways.'

Incorporating Narrative and Storytelling Aspects By incorporating the narrative and storytelling aspects of discourse, strategy-as-practice studies provide detailed accounts of an agentic self and doings in an organization, still missing out on moral human agency. The organization displays itself as a discursive space constituted by the telling and re-telling of stories (Brown, Humphreys and Gurney 2005). As a biograph-ical method, narrative allows for a sequential account of events and the positioning of the individual practitioner in a sociohistorical context (Rouleau 2015) although not in an ethical-moral context. As the stuff of ethnography, stories contribute descriptions of situated actions and interactions, sociality and meaning (Cunliffe 2015). A narrative is described as intrinsically linking 'the "What?" the "How?" and the "Who?" of strategy practice' (Balogun, Beech and Johnson 2015: 452), encompassing several levels of description. A multilevel approach, inspired by Czarniawska (1997), includes the meta-conversation at the organizational level, that is, the logic that directs interactions and activities and legitimizes power relations, and the individual level at which organizational members construct and perpetuate their identities, knowledge and activities through the spoken word (De La Ville and Mounoud 2015).

Through the use of narratives of practices an experiential truth is provided (Rouleau 2015). In relation to role and identity, narrating an experience 'means that the *practitioner* (storyteller) has to cut the self and others in roles and account for the limits and possibilities of these roles', as Balogun, Beech and Johnson (2015: 452, emphasis in original) explain. And, because of disruption of smooth lines of narrative, oscilla-tion of expected and unexpected identity is noticeable. Beech and Johnson (2005) acknowledge that changes in organizational style inter-relate with personal emotional identity changes. A person cast as a hero could transform to an anti-hero, as happens when the hero-identity does not conform to what is expected. An ideal would be that people make sense of strategic change through a coherent and credible narrative and identity. Where polyphony is accepted, several voices make themselves heard as in a musical fugue (Ericson 2007, 2008). Antenarrative as in before narrative, suspending time-sequence, coherence and closure

(Boje 2001) then becomes a more suitable description, allowing for fragmentation and multi-voiced storytelling (Ericson 2010), but a moral voice is not heardIn relation to polyphony, heteroglossia (*raznorečie*) permits a social diversity of speech types and social voices (Bakhtin 1981). On the basis of Bakhtin's dialogism, Helin (2011) illustrates the heteroglot nature of utterance and that at any given time and place an utterance has a certain meaning. Through heteroglot language practices, identity is continually made and remade. And, if we treat the whole world as a text to be read and language as symbols, we 'have no direct referential relationship to the referents, the signified, or objects in the real world', purport Chan and Garrick (2002: 689). Then 'truth' is an enacted effect of discourse, and agency tends to dissolve into many selves, as expressed by the Chilean poet and Nobel laureate (1971) with the pen name Pablo Neruda (in DeGroat 2016: 77): 'Of the many men whom I am, whom we are, I cannot settle on a single one. They are lost to me under the cover of clothing. They have departed for another city.' If one of these many narrating selves allowed in polyphonic and heteroglot language practices is a moral self, we still do not know.

In Connection with Non-human Agency Human agency exposed through discursive practices closely connects with non-human agencies such as those performed by tools, locations, spatial arrangements, financial security and emotions (Balogun *et al.* 2014; Beech and Johnson 2005; Cooren *et al.* 2015). However, these connections do not reveal how morality is expressed and effectuated. In consideration of human and non-human agencies, Lê and Spee (2015) present communication, technology and sensemaking approaches. The communication approach encompasses 'as agents anyone or anything that makes a difference in a given situation' (Cooren *et al.* 2015: 377). Rejecting the dualisms of human and object, micro and macro, the technology approach highlights the interwoven relationship of human and technology. Studies employing this approach elicit a human agency enacted in response to material agency exercised by technology and organizational routines (D'Adderio 2008; Leonardi 2011). Shedding light on the epistemic culture that foregrounds the 'machinery' of knowing, Kaplan (2011) treats Power Point as a technology mobilized in discursive practice. Through a focus on marketization, Çalişkan and Callon (2010) highlight dynamics of a sociotechnical agreement as a form of economization. From the technology approach, then, a market is produced by economists and traders and exists as an aggregation of actions. The sensemaking approach centres on how material objects interact with users' interpretive processes, the role the objects play in these processes and the outcomes rendered.

Bordering on actor–network theory, Chapman, Chua and Mahama (2015) too jumble the human and the non-human together. Human agency and non-human agency are recursively implicated; they use each other to build hybridicity. But their 'influence is rather disproportionate because human agency always has a "head status" while material agency has a "complement status"', submits Leonardi (2011: 150). As practices are inherently sociomaterial we need to move beyond preoccupations of a fixed, demarcating and separating technology from human agency, 'taking seriously notions of distributed agencies, sociomaterial practices, and performative relations as these play in organizational realities', Orlikowski and Scott (2008: 466) assert. Also from the perspective of Tsoukas (2015) human agency is exercised in the context of sociomaterial practices. He conceives of sociomaterial practice as non-deliberate acting and internalized style of practical coping with agency performed against a teleological (teleo-affective) structure. When faced with interruption and trouble, explicit awareness takes over, however, and the agent starts acting deliberately. In such a situation a subject–object polarity is displayed, according to Tsoukas (2015). What the moral implications are when incorporating sociomateriality is not discussed, however.

Extending the Focus to Moral Human Agency

As acknowledged in this chapter, without a concern for morality, strategy-as-practice research directs much attention to agency at the micro level, putting agency into a duality relationship with structure at the macro level. The duality of agency and structure incorporates performative and ostensive aspects without engaging moral action. Not sensitized to the importance of developing an understanding of moral human agency, practice-based studies also introduce us to agents involved in sensemaking, discourse and sociomaterial activities. Discussions around ethical and moral issues are rather confined within business ethics, CSR and stakeholder research, promoting little cross-fertilization between this research and strategy-as-practice research. 'An increasing attention to questions of ethics in the management of business provides an unusually propitious moment for cross-fertilization', Elms *et al.* (2010: 412) argue. They propose that strategy-as-practice scholars engage with and contribute to the interlocution of strategy and ethics. With reference to Clegg, Kornberger and Rhodes (2007), they suggest a focus on business ethics as practice and an examination of how ethics are embedded in practice.

Strategy-as-practice scholars too are advised to explore the role social and moral norms play in business practices (Elms *et al.* 2010).

Studies of strategy-as-practice should then not obscure relationships between strategy and ethics but give relief to human agency in its ethical-oriented practical expressions. As the chapter indicates, largely missing in strategy-as-practice research is a focus on how agency in association with morality, lived in relation to the Other – between practitioners – unfolds in strategy practising. 'Practising' suggests a fluid and open-ended process (Tsoukas and Chia 2002) that constitutes a variety of activities through which morality is articulated and actualized (Chapter 1). Yet, mainly imbued with the conceptual categories of the dominant building worldview (Chia and Rasche 2015; De la Ville and Mounoud 2015), strategy-as-practice studies rely on the assumptions that the individual is a discrete bounded entity and that mental representations precede meaningful action. Practice is approached from the outside. This implicates a 'scientific rationality' that presents features of a pregiven world (Sandberg and Tsoukas 2011: 353).

In contrast with the building worldview, the dwelling worldview, informed by Heideggerian phenomenology, holds that practitioner and practice are mutually constitutive (Chia 2004; Chia and Holt 2006; Chia and MacKay 2007; Chia and Rasche 2015). 'Heidegger showed that the epistemological subject-object relation is not our most basic way of relating to the world but, rather, is derived from a more fundamental way of existence that of being-in-the world', explain Sandberg and Tsoukas (2011: 343). Affording a performative treatment, this existence implies no analytical division among practitioner, praxis and practice. Performative treatment is directly connected to lived experience (Tsoukas and Chia 2002). 'Lived experience' entails a being-in-the-world view which means that we are imbricated in and intrinsically entwined with the world (Chia and Holt 2006; Sandberg and Dall'Alba 2009) and that 'each individual being "becomes" through proximity and encounters with other individual beings' (La Jevic and Springgay 2008: 84). A being-in-the-world view takes entwinement as the primary mode of existence, which 'means that for something to be, it needs to show up as something – namely, as part of a meaningful relational totality with other beings', Sandberg and Tsoukas (2011: 343) maintain.

A focus on moral human agency also requires attention to moral philosophical thinking. Moral philosophy is an ancient discipline but we should not forget about it when attempting to advance our understanding of strategy (Singer 1994). The idea deeply rooted in the traditions of Western philosophy is that human action is 'initiated only after meaningful goals have been set in the cognized world and then – in a separate act of will – the decision to pursue such goals has been taken' (Joas 1996: 157). This view of action, largely articulated in contemporary strategy-as-practice research, reflects Enlightenment thinking of the seventeenth and eighteenth centuries, which, in turn, builds on ancient Greek philosophy arising in the fourth and third centuries BC. Moral philosophical glimpses, provided next, inspire an extension of the focus to moral human agency and propose also a move beyond organizational-level descriptions and duality-based frameworks of agency and structure.

3   Under the Influence of the Old Cosmology

Our present-day modernist understanding of agency and structure bears traces of past-day Enlightenment thinkers, who under the influence of the old cosmology, as represented by Greek philosophers such as Plato (428–348 BC) and Aristotle (384–322 BC), pronounced a dualistic stance toward agency and structure. We must be reminded that the Greek philosophical tradition and its inheritors exhibited strong interest in ethics and morality and that strategy-as-practice research can benefit from addressing this interest. It is essential not to overlook or downplay moral-philosophical reasoning of bygone centuries when attempting to put morality substance into the concept of human agency. We cannot focus strictly on the level of morality in relation to a business. In Franck's (2014: 463) words:

Typically, studies of ethics in business finds morals existing in the form of externally configured yard sticks, like principles, standards, and regulations, against which individuals are assured to employ deliberate moral reasoning to clarify, assess, and manage their behaviors. But from within, ethics is that conditions, from beneath which you can't apply any yardstick, and you can't decide whether someone is or is not ethical.

There must be an awareness of morality in close relation to Ricoeur's (1992) 'ethical aim', which makes it necessary to include moral-philosophical reflections. Ethics is known as moral philosophy (Shafer-Landau 2012) and contrary to morality it is not decisional; 'there is nothing dogmatic about ethics. Because ethics is like breathing for Ricoeur, it is therefore not decisional', accentuates Franck (2014: 463).

The chapter begins by directing attention to Plato's (2000) agent for whom the ruling principle of reason derives from an unchanging cosmic order and continues through a focus on Aristotle's (2011) notion of virtue and on moral ideas and concepts developed in the spirit of the Enlightenment. By bringing the iterational, projective and practical-evaluative dimensions into the discussion of agency and structure, a temporal-relational perspective of moral agency is developed (Emirbayer and Mische 1998). A temporal-relational perspective reaches beyond agency–structure dualities, engaging moral practising in a being-in-the-world mode of interpretation and understanding. Between the old cosmology and the temporal relational, the morality vocabulary broadens, inspiring us to illustrate and distinguish between shades of meaning of morality.

Traced from Plato and Aristotle

Plato's (2000) teleological perspective assumes reason to be the ruling principle, applied by an agent who aims for the good in an absolute sense. Reason is 'the faculty which determines not only what are the proper means for attaining any end, but also what ends are fit to be pursued, and what degree of relative value we ought to put upon each', Adam Smith (1723–1790) (1976: 267) clarifies. The vision of the absolute good, encompassing all partial goods, is at the very centre of Plato's philosophy which manifests the idea of God (Taylor 1989). Moral agency, normatively conditioned by an unchanging cosmic and divine order, represents the same pattern as the good state and is characterized by the four virtues, wisdom, courage, temperance and justice. Wisdom is the most complete form of knowledge. Courage is the ability to preserve an opinion 'whether under the influence of desire or pain' (Plato 2000: 99). Temperance is associated with harmony and symphony and implies control over pleasures and desires. The virtue of justice is more complex; connected to the excellence of the agent's soul it combines wisdom, courage and temperance.

From the viewpoint of Plato (2000), for the one who is wise, courageous and temperate, thus the ruling principle is reason and this is a true account also for a community conceived of as the state. In the interest of the state, both men and women should be as good as possible and in their pursuit of just action express wisdom, courage and temperance. Plato (2000: 131) adds, 'The community of wives and children among our citizens is clearly the source of the greatest good to the State.' Justice, connected to the excellence of the soul, imparts harmony and friendship, whereas injustice creates division and hatred. The soul is 'considered as something like a little state or republic', Smith (1976: 267) comments.

Concurring with Plato, the disciple Aristotle (2011) puts forward the argument that everyone and everything aim for the good. 'But the good is spoken of in relation to *what* something is, and in relation to what *sort* of thing it is, and as regards its *relation* to something' (Aristotle 2011: 8, emphasis in original). From a teleological viewpoint, also to Aristotle there is an awareness of a universal rational principle inherent in a cosmic unchanging order, but greater emphasis is laid upon the practical life. He makes justice in the sense of 'complete virtue' a key for an understanding of how a person should act. On the basis of contemplation (*theoria*) of the providential order and practical wisdom (*phronesis*), a practically wise person knows how to act virtuously and is, accordingly, capable of distinguishing between what is just and unjust to do. 'Concerning justice and injustice, we must examine what sort of actions they happen to be concerned with, as well as what sort of mean justice is and of what things the just is a middle term', clarifies Aristotle (2011: 90).

The golden mean (*mesotēs*) serves as a just measure, which requires a morally virtuous agent to keep to the middle of two opposed vices, one related to excess, the other to deficiency. Exemplified, the moral virtue of generosity is a middle course between wastefulness and stinginess, the moral virtue of kindness suggests a balance of self-respect and empathy, and the moral virtue of courage defines the middle of cowardness and recklessness. In company with Aristotle (2011) we thus note that *theoria* and *phronesis* define moral human agency and are constitutive of the human good in the sense of justice, intrinsically entwined with moral virtue determined by the criterion of *mesotēs*. The structuring principle for the teleological practice, advocated by Aristotle, is ultimately the good life associated with happiness – the highest value in life. However, this suggests a paradox, which Aristotle did not resolve, acknowledges Ricoeur (1992). Without hierarchically arranging the finalities embraced by the structuring principle, it is difficult to make the right virtuous practice an end in itself while aiming at an ulterior end.

In the Spirit of Enlightenment

Inspired by Aristotle, the Stoics stressed human rational capability. The Stoics, as represented by philosophers such a Seneca (4 BC–65), Epictetus (55–135), Cicero (106–43 BC) and the Emperor Marcus Aurelius (121–180) (Stanford Encyclopedia of Philosophy 2016), insisted that 'their physics was the ground of their ethics' (Taylor 1989: 126). Although having a vision of the providence of God, they rejected the value of contemplating a higher order, arguing that man is a rational animal and reason intrinsically practical. Centuries later, reminiscent of Stoic thinking, René Descartes (1596–1650) (1968: 15) expresses the view that ethics is founded on physics and by questioning the philosophy of Aristotle for providing 'the means of talking about all and everything in terms of probabilities', he ascribes morality to a human agent, disengaged from the world and the body. While not having the intention to dishonour Aristotle, Descartes announces the ambition to become the

Aristotle of the Modern Age, supplying the true principles by which an agent arrives at wisdom. Underlying the ethics of Descartes, that is, the Cartesian ethics, the notion of *cogito* designates a self-mastery of reason.

Cartesian ethics prescribes a method we can use for developing our capacity for rational control of elements in our lives. Based on deductive reasoning, the method outlines four rules. The first rule implies intuition by which one knows the fundamental truths of things. According to Descartes (1968: 16) intuition refers to 'the use of the pure lights of the mind as opposed to the evidence of the senses or of the imagination.' The second rule is analysis, requiring a decomposition of complex problems into more simple components. The third is synthesis, by which the truths deduced through the applications of the two previous rules are joined together. The fourth rule emphasizes the principle of *cogito* by which Descartes assured a clear and distinct conception of physical existence.

Disengaging from the world and the body, the Cartesian intention is thus to arrive at certainty and make use of a moral code in accordance with four maxims. The first is to obey laws and customs of one's country while pronouncing a belief in God. The second is to be firm and resolute in actions, not changing direction for weak reasons. The third maxim implies preventing oneself from desiring unobtainable things, always trying to 'escape the sway of Fortune' and conquer oneself through meditation (Descartes 1968: 48). The moral code concludes with the satisfaction of making use of the deductive four-rule method, cultivating reason and discerning true from false for achieving certainty.

Worth noting is that Augustine (354–430) was the inventor of the argument known as *cogito*, Latin for 'I think', positing that we become aware of our awareness, aware of the world and how we experience our experience from a first-person standpoint. Augustine too embraced the Platonic distinction between the bodily and the non-bodily, and the cosmic eternal and the practical. Taylor (1989: 128) summarizes: 'For Augustine as for Plato, the vision of cosmic order is the vision of reason, and for the both of them, the good of human involves their seeing and loving this order ... For the whole moral condition of the soul depends ultimately on what it attends to and loves.' Influenced by Augustine, Descartes (1968: 19) places the human agent at the centre; as a thinking thing, closely united with the non-thinking body, the human agent utters the words 'I think therefore I am' (*Cogito ergo sum*) to announce and assure existence.

Rational Self-Interest Highlighted

The capacity of human beings to shape external circumstances, on the basis of rational self-interest, continued to play a crucial role for the conceptualization of moral agency among social thinkers such as John Locke (1632–1704), Jeremy Bentham (1748–1832) and John Stuart Mill (1806–1873), as Emirbayer and Mische (1998) point out. From the viewpoint of Locke (2008: 134) reason 'stands for a Faculty in Man, That Faculty, whereby Man is supposed to be distinguished from Beasts, and wherein it is evident he much surpasses them.' He introduced the punctual self, maintaining that ideas are produced in the mind of a human agent through operations of particles and processes of associations. As opposed to the Cartesian view of human mind already imprinted with certain ideas about God, soul and existence, the Lockean view holds that human mind is a blank state, a tabula rasa. Hence, there are no innate moral principles the soul receives in its very first being and no divine truth serving as a basis for morality. Things are good or evil, only in reference to the person's own experience of pleasure and pain.

To Locke (2008), the human will (as distinguished from desire) is an action, and freedom is a power of acting and not acting. Action is annexed to an individual agent, the mind of whom is equipped with senses, perception and reason. With Locke the view developed that we are morally rational if we allow ourselves to act in accordance with the law of nature. Nature has a law that restrains us from hurting one another. Locke (2008: 7) explains: 'In transgressing the law of nature, the offender declares himself to live by another rule than that of reason and common equity.' 'Locke's person is the moral agent who takes responsibility for his acts in the light of future retribution. The abstracted picture of the self faithfully reflects his ideal of responsible agency', concludes Taylor (1989: 173).

Locke (2008) inspired the emergence of Deism, the central idea of which is 'that God relates to humans as rational beings, that God's purpose fully respects humans' autonomous reason' (Taylor 1989: 245). Thus there was no possibility for God's direct invention in the world. Deism prepared the way for a mechanistic view of universe influenced by Newton's (1642–1727) cosmology. A mechanized scientific view of the world conjoined with a rational control view of independent and self-influenced Enlightenment thinking. 'Thus if we follow the theme of self-control through the vicissitudes of our Western tradition, we find a very profound transmutation, all the way from the hegemony of reason as a vision of cosmic order to the notion of a punctual disengaged subject exercising instrumental control' (Taylor 1989: 174).

Now, living according to reason and nature meant living 'according to the design of things' (Taylor 1989: 279). Rationality was regarded to form procedurally in line with specific standards. Utilitarianism developed and influenced the emergence of other forms of utilitarianism (consequentialism) (Shafer-Landau 2012). For Bentham (1988) and Mill (1998), representing classic utilitarianism, the merit of an action depends on the moral rightness of its actual results in terms of utility and as maintained, nature should be managed for the benefit of humans. The ultimate standard of morality originates in the so-called optimific principle of utility, according to which the agent should choose the action that maximizes well-being. Two masters govern us in all we do; these are pain and pleasure, which are 'produced in men's minds by the action of certain causes', Bentham (1988: 43) informs us.

Utility is 'that property in any object, whereby it tends to produce benefit, advantage, pleasure, good, or happiness' (Bentham 1988: 2). This entails that any 'instance of promise keeping, truth telling, or kindness that fails to be optimific is *immoral*" (Shafer-Landau 2012: 144, emphasis in original). When comparing the amount of benefit and harm of an action, the ratio of benefit to harm should be as great as possible. Yet one should not take this too seriously, Shafer-Landau (2012) remarks, because the ability to give concrete advice might be lost in complex situations when we are unable to assess the amount of benefit and harm done by an action. Moreover, results can occur long decades or even centuries after the action took place.

In addition to utility, happiness, desire and satisfaction intimately relate to the good. Ever since the days of Epicurus (341–270 BC), hedonism has been occupied with the question of how to achieve happiness, a prerequisite for a good life filled with pleasure and free of pain (Shafer-Landau 2012). Rather than physical pleasures, happiness in the form of an inner state of peace, intellectual and artistic pleasure is seen as worth pursuing for its own sake, Mill (1998) argues. The intrinsic value of happiness insists on the importance of avoiding pain and removing burdens that make life miserable. Utility as happiness is the directive rule of human conduct. As Mill (1998: 55) puts it: 'The creed which accepts as the foundation of morals, utility, or the Greatest Happiness Principle, holds that actions are right in proportion as they tend to promote happiness, wrong as they tend to produce the reverse of happiness. By happiness is intended pleasure, and the absence of pain; by unhappiness, pain, and privation of pleasure.'

Desire satisfaction theorists hold that an agent has the freedom to envision a good life but is unable to deal with situations of conflicting desires and assess whether one desire is better than another (Shafer-Landau 2012). Only informed and self-guarding desires can improve a person's life. Our desires should then not be based on false beliefs, and we should be aware that getting what we actually want might not be essential to the creation of a good life. In close relation to desire theorists, psychological egoist theorists maintain that self-interest serves morality. In the absence of altruism every action is then done for personal gains and benefits. But as Shafer-Landau (2012: 113) expressively comments: 'My right to life or to free speech is worthless if other people are allowed to kill me or shut me up whenever it serves their interests to do so.'

A number of reactions to the conception of morality associated with rational self-interest led to an ethics of nature, articulated by Jean-Jacques Rousseau (1712–1778), a universally adapted law of morality, developed by Immanuel Kant (1724–1804) and an idea of a common good, proposed by Hutcheson (2007) and Smith (1976) in connection with sympathy and passion.

An Ethics of Nature, a Law of Morality and a Common Good

Unlike Locke (2008), Rousseau considers the social environment to be of minor importance for the inner growth of an individual, who is urged not to become enslaved by conventions and social approval (Crain 1992). In the words of Rousseau (2003: 1): 'Everything is good as it comes from the hands of the Author of Nature, but everything degenerates in the hands of man.' Idealizing a simple natural life, Rousseau advocates a pantheistic view, picturing nature as a vast network of interlocking beings and as the prime moral source, Taylor (1989) clarifies.

With the breakdown of the idea of a larger providential structure as an objective rational order, the understanding that nature resonates within us was enhanced. To Rousseau, feelings count as instincts that provide us with knowledge of what is good and evil, right and wrong, with nature conceived as 'a great keyboard on which our highest sentiments are played out' (Taylor 1989: 297). Expanding on this view, leaving out feelings, impulses and inclinations, Kant (1956) moved the law of morality to the fore. The word *vernüftig* used by Kant defines reason as self-consciousness, covering the terms 'reasonable' and 'rational', informs Rawls (2000: 164). Intrinsically tied to duty, a deontological perspective of morality formed. As opposed to the teleological perspective, the deontological refers to a moral agency rooted in will in relation to law.

Kant (1956) dichotomizes reality into two orders, one consisting of conditioned activity and the other of unconditioned normative activity. There is an unconditioned and objective moral standard according to which a rational moral agent ought to act. In other words, the a priori part of ethics, as opposed to the practical part, concerns duty and must not be confused with self-interest. The deontological perspective thus implies that an action done from duty has moral worth and is based on a maxim that can be raised to the level of a universal law. This maxim is presented by the formula '*Act only on that maxim through which you can at the same time will that it should become a universal law*' (Kant 1956: 30, emphasis in original). A universal law, independent of any influence of senses and assigned unconditioned value, is designated 'categorical imperative'. In Kant's view, our good will is determined by the universal and constraining aspect of duty, articulated by the categorical imperative. The Kantian will is thought of as a power only found in rational beings who are treated not as means, but as ends in themselves.

A morally good human being does not act from passion or self-interest, as Kant (1956) asserts. From the perspective of Hutcheson (2007: 29, emphasis in original), a morally good human being also shows good will towards the Other, expressing joy and sorrow: 'when good is obtained as evil avoided, arises *Joy* when good is lost or evil befallen us, *Sorrow*.' Human nature consists of soul and body by the senses of which we express good and evil. We are able to 'discern what is graceful, becoming, beautiful and honourable in the affections of the soul in our conduct of life, our words and action' (Hutcheson 2007: 35). The soul presents us with the powers of understanding and of will. 'The former contains all the powers which aim at knowledge; the other all our desires [pursuing happiness and eschewing misery]', Hutcheson (2007: 25) explains. Understanding operates through external senses, which depend on the body, and internal senses, which refer to conscience of our state of mind. Conscience, counted as virtue, is the noblest and most divine of all our senses.

Also of note, Hutcheson (2007: 33) puts forward the argument that we should promote the common good of all: 'we rejoice in the prosperity of others, and sorrow with them in their misfortunes.' By means of sympathy, conceived of as a fellow-feeling, we share our pleasures with others when showing good will towards them. Duty is consequently performed towards the Other. 'Virtue' is then implied in a common interest expressed through mutual love, good will and kind offices. 'All men who have not quite divested themselves of humanity, and taken up the temper of savage beasts, must feel that without mutual love, good-will and kind offices, we can enjoy no happiness; and that solitude, even in the greatest affluence of external things, must be miserable', Hutcheson (2007: 82) posits. Smith (1976: 28), the disciple of Hutcheson, also urges us to put ourselves in the situation of others and produce harmony of sentiments and passion, distinguishing between decent passions such as generosity, kindness and compassion, and indecent passions arising from 'appetites which take their origin from the body.' Citing the Stoic philosopher Cicero, Smith (1976: 140–141) contends that man 'ought to regard himself, not as something separated and detached, but as a citizen of the world, a member of the vast common wealth of nature.'

Less focused on the rational punctual self, both Hutcheson (2007) and Smith (1976) hold that morality concerns social interaction and what occurs between human beings. We should view ourselves not in the light in which our own selfish passions are apt to place us, but in the light in which any other citizen of the world views us. Akin to corporate (Hemphill 2004) and global citizenships (Logsdon and Wood 2005) there are qualities of propriety or impropriety and merit or demerit to agency that amount to 'double sympathy'. According to Hutcheson (2007: 73), this implies:

when to the beneficent tendency of the action is joined the propriety of the affection from which it proceeds, when we entirely sympathize and go along with the motives of the agent, the love which we conceive for him upon his own account, enhances and enlivens our fellow-feeling with the gratitude of those who owe their propriety to his good conduct.

Other social thinkers also direct attention to a multidimensional agency concept in consideration of social interaction and betweenness. They challenge the Kantian dichotomy of the conditioned and unconditioned dimensions of agency, yet with little interest dedicated to temporality. In the twentieth century, we meet scholars who explicitly address the Kantian dichotomized reality. Parson (1968), Coleman (1990) and Alexander (1988), for example, try to overcome this dichotomy by inter-relating purposive activity at the micro level with systemic interdepend-ence at the macro level, linking together and even synthesizing the conditioned and unconditioned dimensions of agency (Emirbayer and Mische 1998). Although they make us aware of a more multidimensional concept of agency, none seems to give considerable attention to temporality.

Parson (1968) does not elaborate on temporality: 'agency remained "outside" time (as in Kant's own conception of the "unconditioned"), while structure remained a spatial category rather than (also) a temporal construction', acknowledge Emirbayer and Mische (1998: 966). Although there is to Kant (1956) transference from the individual agent to an imaginary all through the proposed universalization of the moral law, there is little focus on temporal relationality. Coleman (1990) dis-cards variable temporal agentic processes, sustaining the difficulty of explaining a transition from the macro to the micro level and from the micro to the macro level. Transitions are matters of institutional design, aggregation and interaction among actors and 'arise through the effects of various actors' actions on other actors' actions. This also leads directly to the question of strategy on the part of authorities and on the part of their opponents', Coleman (1990: 500) comments. By stressing the normative and downplaying the constitutive features of invention, Alexander (1988) too fails to include temporality in agency (Emirbayer and Mische 1998). To give temporality a more salient role, the iterational, projective and practical-evaluative dimensions of activity are brought into the discussion.

Bringing in the Iterational, Projective and Practical-Evaluative

Practice suggests a nexus of activities (Schatzki 1996) that is constituted of varying temporal-relational social contexts, mediating human experience. Drawing on Mead's (1932) work, Emirbayer and Mische (1998: 968, emphasis in original) purport that 'human experience of temporality is based in the *social* character of emergence, that is, in the passage from the old to the new, and in the interrelated changes occurring throughout the various situational contexts within which human beings are embedded.' The term 'sociality', coined by Mead (1932), refers to the capacity of being several things at once and the term 'social' implies readjustment. An outstanding illustration of this is found in ecology. According to Mead (1932: 73): 'There is an answer in the community in the meadow or the forest to the entrance of any new form, if that form can survive.' By introducing the iterational, projective and practical-evaluative dimensions into a discussion of agency, the opportunity arises to develop an understanding concerned with a temporal unfolding of moral human agency. We need also to recognize that temporality does not necessitate linearity and context does not always exist ready to *embed* a social phenomenon but forms as human agents relate to others and interact (Ericson 2014). This has implications for our understanding of the agency–structure duality, predominantly applied in strategy-as-practice research (Chapter 2).

The iterational dimension assigns to activity an almost unreflective, tacit and taken-for-granted character. It builds on corporeal, affective and cognitive experiences that are structured and institutionalized through repetition and habit, variously termed routine, disposition, typification and tradition (Emirbayer and Mische 1998). These experiences condition present activity, influencing and even stabilizing the way in which agents recall, attend to and reactivate a past. Experiences of a past alert agents to certain elements of emerging situations, providing them with relatively reliable knowledge of social relationships that help to sustain expectations about continuity of activity. When promoting temporal continuity, agents tend to exercise deliberative capacity, smoothing over differences between situations by assimilating new experiences to the old and relying on generalizations that recognize similarities between past and present situations. Deliberative capacity refers to 'the capacity to get hold of the conditions of future conduct as these are found in the organized responses we have formed, and so construct our pasts in anticipation of that future' (Mead 1932: 76).

By challenging the rational and inherently teleological means–ends and normative presuppositions of deliberative capacity, Joas (1996) accentuates a conception of agency that allows for agents' innovative and critical inventions. Habit is also inherently plastic and edicable, Emirbayer and Mische (1998) agree. Not devoid of agency, habitual and repetitive activity does not produce a fixed and mechanical reaction to stimuli (Camic 1986). Employing a duality-based approach, Giddens (1979) maintains that agency and structure are mutually constitutive, allowing room for change. His conception of structuration introduces temporality. Time is identified with change but also with stability as stability implies continuity over time. Less rigid than a dichotomization of agency and structure, presented as a dualism composed of two opposing poles, the duality bridges and interrelates the agentic purposive at the micro level and the routinized normative at the macro level. By means of *habitus* and field, Bourdieu (1990) accentuates the interplay between agency and structure, giving room for readjustment in the form of regulated improvization that is needed for objective structures to be reproduced. *Habitus* can be seen as 'a programme that produces behavior in accordance with certain rules but also dependent on the input from the environment. In this sense, the habitus is truly creative', summarizes Weik (2014: 107).

Although a duality of agency and structure reconciles the antagonism between the polarized elements, there can still be a tendency to understand one side through the other and emphasize one side at the expense of the other (Jackson 1999; Knights 1997). To both Giddens (1979) and Bourdieu (1990) the taken-for-granted structural features of reality seem to play a more salient role than engagement of the future (Mische 2009). A duality much like a dualism reflects a form of determinism that might violate the interactive character of agency and structure (Ericson 2004). By opening up for creative and future-oriented human activity the deterministic features of the agency–structure duality weaken. In Joas's (1996: 158) words: 'The world exists not simply as an external counterpart to our internal self, but in the form of possible actions.'

On the basis of a philosophical and pragmatist understanding of human action, Joas (1996) sees creativity as profoundly related to life and intelligence. Life refers to the metaphysical level and intelligence concerns the practical level. The pragmatist understanding of human action connects intelligence to concrete reconstruction and concerns the recognition and realization of possibilities inherent in the world. Even relatively unreflective action could have its own moment of creativity as 'typification and routinization of experience are active processes entailing selective reactivation of received structures within expected situations, dynamic transaction between actor and situation', contend Emirbayer and Mische (1998: 976). Although often oriented to a past, processes of iteration then shade over into the more future-oriented projective dimension and into the practical-evaluative dimension of agency that can be both future- and past-oriented.

While the iterational dimension has received much attention in philosophy and sociological theory, the projective dimension has been largely ignored. Most studies have focused on a sequential time perspective 'limited by overly behavioral and correlational assumptions' (Emirbayer and Mische 1998: 991). Projectivity is a fundamental dimension of human agency. Characterized by an experimental relationship with the future, it opens up to imaginative recomposition of past experiences and structures. Projective action is marked by indeterminacy with both means and ends temporally evolving (Schutz 1967). Highlighting the intersubjective aspect of projectivity, Mead (1932) points to the imaginative capacity of an agent, who along with others is able to engage in coordinating efforts while dealing with conflicts and solving problems.

A more concrete outline of projectivity accounts for activities in terms of anticipatory identification, narrative construction, symbolic recomposition, hypothetical resolution and experimental enactment (Emirbayer and Mische 1998). Anticipatory identification concerns continual reevaluation of typifications and established repertories of action. Closely related to narrative construction, a possible representation of anticipatory identification is through stories and plots. A story serves as a temporal framing and a plot provides structure to a story by combining elements (events) into a whole (Polkinghorne 1988). Symbolic recomposition is encouraged by agents involved in projective imagination by means of scenarios and future trajectories for action. Hypothetical resolution refers to the ways in which an agent responds to different lived conflicts. It entails experimental enactment; through social dramas an agent might reinforce or change ritually the social order and the social role.

Also the practical-evaluative dimension in its future and past orientation has received limited interest in prior research of action and in moral philosophy. According to Emirbayer and Mische (1998) this dimension stresses the communicative transactional processes of adjusting norms, routines and disposition to the exigencies of changing lived situations. Practical evaluation is associated with problematization, characterization, deliberation and decision making. Problematization refers to ambiguous and unresolved situations, and characterization to a situation that calls for an iterational activity. Characterization thus accounts for a past that applies to present exercise of routines and typifications. Deliberation suggests dealing with the ambiguity of the situation at hand when aiming towards a decision. While a decision does not always lend itself to easy formulation, it might be articulated retrospectively and be a matter of continuous present adoption to changing circumstances. Through the execution of a decision, a movement is marked towards concrete actions that make practical evaluation complete.

Practical evaluation also suggests that agents can engage in temporal improvization through deliberate control of intervals between events and actions, advancing their interests by choosing the right time for action (Emirbayer and Mische 1998). They can resist and subvert practice and through authorized means of action such as strikes and demonstrations, so-called repertoires of contention, express their opinions and oppose a decision. In situations lacking clear expectations for action, opportunity for practical evaluation arises through local or prudential action. This implies that agents acquire roles in interactions with others and depending on the situation at hand appropriate actions are taken. In political decision making, agents are confronted with multiple possibilities of action and the testing of limits of a situation. The performance of an agent can be a potent way of exercising power but always in the context of organizational and institutional constraints. In agreement with Emirbayer and Mische (1998), Feldman and Pentland (2003) hold that organizational routines allow for individuals' active engagement in practices and interpretations of agency with various forms of structures. A reflexive self-monitoring agency implicates a participant's apparent choice of action, adds Giddens (1979).

Moving beyond the Modernistic Language of Agency and Structure

The iterational, projective and practical-evaluative dimensions form a temporal-relational perspective that applies to practitioners' in-betweens. It attributes to experience of temporality a social character in recognition of social interactions that help to sustain some stability and continuity of actions but do not necessarily require linearity. Referring to Emirbayer and Mische (1998), Kaplan and Orlikowski (2013) point to temporal work that only builds on a chronology. Yet practitioners can use a temporal-relational understanding to develop a capacity to shape their present responses to an emerging future while reconstructing their past in anticipation of a future. There is simultaneity between present future-oriented and present past-oriented movements (Ericson 2014).

A temporal-relational interpretation and understanding reach beyond the modernistic two-category language of agency and structure that builds on a representational view of reality to a non-representational alternative concerned with the individual's entwinement with the world. Akin to the dwelling worldview, directly linked to lived experience, such interpretation and understanding elicit an awareness that practising in terms of activities extends from the practitioners' existential situations (Chia 2004; Chia and Holt 2006) (Chapter 2). The iterational, projective and practical-evaluative dimensions accentuate 'social' and 'sociality' (Mead 1932). Hence, there is no single inward-looking agent rationally capable of reaching a state of happiness, in solitude governed by reason and a vision of self-accruing advantages. Nor is there an agent solely governed by the structure of providence or the law of nature, capable of maximizing well-being by estimating the ratio of benefit and harm of an action, advancing a pantheistic idea of morality or immersing in good will acting out of duty on a maxim raised to the level of universal law.

Next, the Löfbergs Group context is presented. As pointed out earlier (Chapter 1), we cannot neglect the beautiful portrait easily accessible in official documents. At the same time, it is important to be aware that the Group context holds a movement towards a context that forms as practitioners interact, expressing and effectuating morality.

4   The Löfbergs Group
A Predefined Coffee Context

The Swedish companies Bröderna Löfberg AB and AB Anders Löfberg AB (a subsidiary to Bröderna Löfberg AB) constitute a group that stands on two pillars, real estate and coffee. This group is wholly owned by the Löfberg family, represented by the members in the third and fourth generations. Since the start-up in 1906, AB Anders Löfberg has steadily grown, expanding its markets outside the national borders. A workforce of 360 employees daily engages in business operations increasingly international in character. Over the last few years, foreign coffee companies have been acquired. Today, AB Anders Löfberg is established as a group of companies and this group is of particular interest in this study and is hereinafter referred to as the Löfbergs Group or simple the group. From 2008, Lars Appelqvist has been the CEO. On January 1, 2015, Kathrine Löfberg assumed the position as Chairman of the Löfbergs Board of Directors, succeeding her father, Anders Löfberg, who had been in that position since 1999. The Löfbergs coffee group comprises the following wholly-owned subsidiaries: Löfbergs Lila AB, Löfbergs Lila AS, Crema Kaffebrenneri AS, Melna Kafija, Löfbergs UK, and Food Brands Group (personal communication, Lars Appelqvist, December 30, 2016; *Annual Report* 2013/2014, 2014/2015).[1]

Löfbergs Lila AB focuses on product development and marketing of Löfbergs coffee and Kobbs tea in the Swedish and Finnish markets; Löfbergs Lila AS and Crema Kaffebrenneri AS market coffee in the Norwegian market; Melna Kafija operates in the markets of Estonia, Latvia and Lithuania. Löfbergs UK offers the coffee brand Green Cup, and the Food Brands Group the brand Percol in the UK market. The coffee group also includes Peter Larsen Kaffe AS, owned at 75 per cent.

---

[1] *Annual Report* 2013/2014 and *Annual Report* 2014/2015 (cited in Chapter 4 and Chapter 5) both refer to AB Anders Löfberg Annual Report with Sustainability Report, covering the financial year that begins on July 1 and concludes on June 30 of the following year.

This company is in charge of product development and marketing of coffee under the brand Peter Larsen Kaffe in the Danish market.

The empirical-theoretical discussion in this chapter ascribes moral agency to the Löfbergs Group. The group gains a nearly thing-like existence when depicted as a functional whole that acts upon and interacts with its external environment in which network partners and other stakeholders reside. A subject–object understanding of organization and environment is thus promoted, operating in favour of ontic concerns (Stefanovic 2000). Here ontic refers to a description of what is already present in terms of a coffee context that prioritizes relationships between units that make up the Löfbergs Group. Predefined, this context serves as a frame of reference for illuminating the relevance of morality, mainly with regard to sustainability and sustainable development. As illustrated, the group is involved in a number of different national and international networks, many of which engage in sustainability work integrated with corporate social responsibility (CSR). Network participation extends through webs of partners, defining a 'good social force' that translates to corporate and global citizenship. The chapter also alludes to the 'green' institutional level at which sustainability work in integration with CSR is given legitimacy. Before closing, it points to the need to move beyond a group-related moral agency and direct attention to moral human agency as it unfolds through practising that constitutes a variety of strategic-oriented activities.

Sustainability and Sustainable Development in Focus

For more than one hundred years, sustainability and the practising of sustainability through sustainable development have been the focus of the Löfberg family, whose vision is briefly stated in the words 'Good moments for future generations', which also include coming generations of coffee farmers, customers and employees, accentuates Kathrine Löfberg, owner, Chairman of the Board of Directors. Additionally, the vision pronounces the will of the Löfbergs Group 'to be regarded the most sustainable coffee group in Europe that with passion, strong brands and the best tasting coffee delivers increased value for our customers and owner' (*Annual Report* 2014/2015: 8) The goal is to have 'the best tasting and most sustainable coffee and through that achieve long-term profitability', CEO Lars Appelqvist (*Annual Report* 2014/2015: 3) adds.

The Löfbergs Group has evolved into one of Europe's most sustainable coffee groups and one of the biggest coffee roasters in the Nordic region with a turnover of approximately SEK 1.7 billion in the financial year 2014/2015 and a production of about 10.5 million coffee cups a day.

The group holds 20 per cent market share in Sweden. 'The coffee market is tough with law margin and fierce competition', reveals the CEO (*Annual Report* 2014/2015: 3). In order to continue promoting sustainable growth while boosting competitiveness, the group has to deal with a number of challenges. Among these, climate changes are essential to address, especially in relation to coffee growing. Coffee is bought directly from countries in South America (67 per cent), Central America (17 per cent), Africa (11 per cent) and Asia (5 per cent) and some of these countries have been severely affected by pests and drought (*Annual Report* 2013/2014, 2014/2015).

Climate researchers paint a rather pessimistic picture, not only in relation to coffee production, but also with respect to interrelated and multilevel changes with unintended consequences on ecosystems and societies worldwide (Adger and Brown 2010). The Industrial Revolution of the 1800s gave rise to a new era, the Anthropocene, which replaced a period of relative stability that under the name of the Holocene endured through around 10,000 years (Rockström 2009). In the anthropogenic era, human activities are seen as the main driver of global environmental change, leading to degradation of rainforests, deserts and marine life (Shrivastava 1995). The atmospheric concentration of carbon dioxide causes abrupt shifts in agricultural systems, threatening the extinction of up to 30 per cent of all mammal, bird and amphibian species (Rockström 2009). Land-use change such as deforestation is strongly related to biodiversity loss. In Mexico, known for an extraordinarily diverse biological richness, deforestation has become a prime concern (Velázquez *et al.* 2003). The growing of monocultures, through which large land areas are cultivated with a single crop, too has significant negative impacts on the ecological systems of the earth, causing water shortage and contamination from pesticide spraying (*Carbon Trade Watch* 2016).

Defined by the World Commission on Environment and Development: Common Future, presented in the Brundtland Report (1987: 43), sustainable development is 'a process of change in which the exploitation of resources, the direction of investments, the orientation of technological development; and institutional change are all in harmony and enhance both current and future potential to meet human needs and aspirations.' This definition was adopted by the United Nations Conference on Environment and Development in Rio de Janeiro in 1992. Other conferences followed, the most recent held in Paris in December 2015, in the pursuit of sustainable development consistently accounting for social and ecological factors. As purported by the Brundtland Report (1987: 7), environment and development are inseparable: 'The "environment" is where we all live and "development" is what we all do in attempting to improve our lot within that abode.'

For development to be sustainable it is 'important to include all sustainability aspects: environmental, social and financial ... We have to talk about the challenges that the planet and its inhabitants face and about the initiatives that we take to contribute to a more sustainable development', emphasizes Eva Eriksson, Sustainability Director (*Annual Report* 2014/2015: 12). A transdisciplinary management perspective is thus preferred for fostering an understanding that human, community and nature are intrinsically entwined (Starkey and Crane 2003). In communication with researchers, participation in research conferences on sustainability, business ethics and CSR, arranged by CTF Service Research Center at Karlstad University, and based on students' master theses that direct attention to the creation of a values-driven sustainable service business (Enquist 2007) and corporate social responsibility in the coffee sector (Mößner 2014; Persson 2008), the Löfbergs Group gains inspiration for applying such a perspective. The diversity, complexity and dynamics of environmental problems cannot be handled by employing intellectual tools from just one single discipline (Hirsh Hadorn *et al.* 2006). Different scientific disciplines need to be integrated and synthesized under the umbrella of transdisciplinarity, acknowledge Connelly, Ketchen and Slater (2011). One must be aware that the future is not adjustable according to company-specific preferences only and that the management has a critical mediating role to play between ecosciences and society (Starkey and Crane 2003). Inherent in the vision, formulated by the Löfberg family, is a future that holds 'a way of doing business that creates profit while avoiding harm to people and the planet' (Connelly, Ketchen and Slater 2011: 86).

Strongly aware of climate changes, the Löfbergs Group carries out socially responsible actions, translating ecological economics through continuously engaging in sustainable development, which also provides a basis for generating profits and competitive advantage. The assertion that sustainability is a source of economic advantage has, however, been questioned by some scholars from the view that the economic character of business insulates business situations from social responsibilities (Elms *et al.* 2010; Klonoski 1991). However, to Connelly, Ketchen and Slater (2011), sustainability is an effective way for a firm to achieve a position of competitive advantage, an argument that the Löfbergs Group accepts. Sustainability is an integral part of the business model. As pronounced by Lars Appelqvist: 'The sustainability work is about profitability, and that is an important part of our business. It strengthens our brand, increases our proceeds and drive costs out of our systems' (*Annual Report* 2013/2014: 3).

The Löfbergs Group participates in a variety of networks, many of which engage in sustainability work integrated with corporate social responsibility. Worth noting is that the importance of promoting CSR was acknowledged right from the start of the Löfbergs business. In the words of Kathrine Löfberg (*Get to Know a Good Coffee* 2013: 4):

My family started importing and selling coffee long before the concept of Corporate Social Responsibility was invented. However, these principles have always been an important part of our business, starting when our great-grandfather committed himself to helping the local poor in the early 20th century. Being part of the wider world and trying to help make it a better place still feels entirely natural.

Corporate Social Responsibility of Continuing Concern

Going back to the beginning of the 1900s, business implications of CSR (see also Chapter 2) were regarded as not very palatable to shareholders. In 1917, Henry Ford's idea that business is a service to society was derided not only by shareholders but also by the court (Lee 2007). One was not convinced that CSR could positively influence the financial performance of an organization. Even in the 1960s, CSR was considered imposing an unfair and costly burden on shareholder wealth. Corporate managers' primary responsibility was considered to be the maximization of shareholder wealth. Friedman (1962) and other 'functionalist fundamentalists' (e.g. Levitt 1983) suggested that 'our society, as it expresses itself through the free market, is committed to a radical pluralism', and that 'a social, political, and economic pluralism is best perceived when major "functional groups" do not encroach on each other's provinces of behavior' (Klonoski 1991: 9). It is worth noting, though, that Bowen (1953), casting light on the social aspect, provided 'the intellectual springboard to reflect on the rapidly changing social environment during the ensuing two decades' (Elms *et al.* 2010: 57). From the viewpoint of Bowen (1953), CSR should be of growing concern to business managers. Yet a breakthrough in the conceptual development of CSR did not come until the late 1970s. Until then, 'CSR was derided as a joke, an oxymoron and a contradiction in terms by the investment and business community', Lee (2007: 53) notes. Carroll (1991: 39) summarizes: 'For the better part of 30 years now, corporate executives have struggled with the issue of the firm's responsibility to its society.'

Not deriding it as a joke or an oxymoron, the Löfbergs Group integrates CSR with sustainability work for spurring profitable growth but also with the intention to contribute in a broader context as reflected by activities the group performs as a member of national and international networks. As Kathrine Löfberg describes (personal communication, June 9, 2015): 'There are a great many networks, carrying out different types of projects nationally and internationally. In Sweden, networks generally encompass actors within the food industry engaging in CSR and sustainability work. The international networks are more oriented towards development projects in coffee producing countries.'

CSR Sweden, Swedish Leadership for Sustainable Development, UNICEF, Coffee Kids, Good for Life Charity, The Swedish Environmental Management Council, the Haga Initiative, International Coffee Partners (ICP), 'Förpacknings- och Tidningsinsamlingen' (FTI; Packaging and Newspaper Collection Service), and Sustainable Food Chain are networks focused on sustainability work, undertaken beyond mere business-related concerns of the Löfbergs Group (*Annual Report* 2013/2014, 2014/2015).

CSR Sweden consists of eighteen member companies and is Sweden's leading business network that in interaction with politicians focuses on corporate social responsibility, including community involvement and development. CSR Sweden, started by the Swedish Jobs and Society Foundation, is the national partner of CSR Europe, which was founded in 1995 in Brussels on the initiative of the European Commission's former president Jacques Delors. CSR Europe, gathering more than 10,000 companies, 'acts as a platform for those businesses looking to enhance sustainable growth and positively contribute to society' (*CSR Europe, About Us* 2015: 1). CSR Europe cooperates with other CSR organizations outside European borders. CSR Sweden, maintaining strong links to CSR Europe, primarily engages in Swedish companies in promoting CSR (*CSR Sweden* 2015).

Swedish Leadership for Sustainable Development consists of approximately twenty-three members, serving as a platform for exchange of knowledge, initiation of new partnerships and projects for poverty reduction and sustainable development. Projects include vocational training in African countries, the reduction of water and chemical use in the textile industry. In line with the UN Sustainable Development Goals, the network builds cross-sectoral partnerships, challenging companies worldwide to advance their positions in sustainability (*Swedish Leadership for Sustainable Development* 2015). The network is administered by SIDA (Swedish International Development Cooperation Agency), a government agency with the mission to allocate aid for reducing poverty in the world. This organization carries out development projects in cooperation with countries in Africa, Asia, Europe and Latin America (*SIDA* 2015).

UNICEF (United Nations International Children's Emergency Fund), founded in 1946, works closely with multi-national corporations and national companies to promote the well-being of every child while also assuring equality for those who are discriminated against. With partners in 190 countries, UNICEF strives to give children the best start in life, promoting their education and creating protective environments. Safe, healthy and well-educated children are a starting point for sustainable development. UNICEF and its partners attend to global work with governments, national and international agencies and the civil society to support life-saving actions at each phase in a child's life and throughout childhood to adulthood. This is done in order to meet the Millennium Development Goals and the norms and standards set by the Convention of the Rights of the Child and the Convention on the Elimination of All Forms of Discrimination against Women (*UNICEF Annual Report* 2015).

Coffee Kids too centres the focus on children. It works with partners in rural coffee-farming communities in Latin America with projects in the areas of education, health care, economic diversification, food security and capacity building. The education projects have given thousands of children the opportunity to study. Through health care projects, women learn to identify and treat illnesses with natural medicines and how to deliver and improve preventive health care. Economic diversification activities in the form of microcredit projects enable women to start up and run their own businesses, ranging from selling vegetables or tortillas to running a midwife clinic or a general store. Food security projects concentrate on backyard gardening, worm composting, grocery stores and nutritional education. Capacity building projects administer technical and administrative training to coffee-growing communities (*Coffee Kids* 2015). As a member of the Good for Life Charity network, the Löfbergs Group also has the opportunity to make life better worldwide, primarily through empowering women to build a sustainable future for their children. The network provides expertise and financial support predominantly in Latin America, Africa and Nepal (*Good for Life Charity* 2015).

The Swedish Environmental Management Council provides environmental and social criteria to be used when purchasing goods and services and establishing work contracts. The criteria are in line with the EU obligations. The emphasis on green public procurement suggests 'a process whereby public authorities seek to procure goods, services and works with a reduced environmental impact throughout their lifecycle when compared to goods, services and works with the same primary function that would otherwise be procured' (*European Commission Environment* 2016: 1).

The Haga Initiative is a network that views climate change as a most critical issue for the future. It pushes the member companies to pursue social responsibility actively through reducing their carbon footprint and prioritizing the creation of a sustainable society. Moreover, it highlights the interrelations between climate strategies and profitability of businesses. Eva Eriksson (personal communication, February 13, 2015), explains:

I participate in that network and we have a number of things in the pipeline. We are committed to reduce our climate impact while also performing well in profitable terms. In some cases, there is potential for businesses to directly make a profit when reducing the climate impact whereas in others, only indirectly or in the long run ... We apply the broader perspective considerate about both short- and long-term consequences of climate changes for planet Earth. The members of the network communicate with Professor Johan Rockström in Environmental Science at Stockholm Resilience Centre ... I meet with so many interesting people who inspire me to learn more about the climate. Being part of this network requires your sincere commitment; admission is contingent on the CEO being actively involved in meetings, pursuing energy efficiency improvements to reach a 40 per cent reduction in greenhouse emission by the year 2020 compared to the 1990 level.

The Haga network was initiated in 2010 by Axfood, Coca-Cola Enterprises Sweden, Fortum Värme, JM, Procter & Gamble Sweden, Stena Recycling, Statoil Fuel & Retail Sweden, and Vasakronan. Then, Lantmännen, Green Cargo, Folksam, HKScan Sweden, Sveaskog, McDonald's, and Löfbergs joined. The eco-park Haga with its Butterfly Museum is situated on Öland, a Swedish island. It is a place where sustainable policies are discussed and goals are set by the member companies (*The Haga Initiative* 2015). Eco-parks are communities of companies working together to improve performance in sustainability areas (Elkington 1998).

Sustainability work is, in addition, promoted by the International Coffee Partners (ICP), a network established in 2001 by four family-owned coffee companies. Today, ICP consists of Löfbergs, Luigi Lavazza, Gustav Paulig, Newmann Kaffee Gruppe, Tchibo, Joh. Johannson Kaffe, and Franck who together with SIDA and GIZ (Deutsche Gesellschaft Zusammenarbeit) engage in improving the coffee farmers' ability to cope with climate changes and boosting competitiveness through increased productivity, product quality and efficiency (see also Chapter 5). Included in this work is strengthening the role of women in different communities (*International Coffee Partners, About Us* 2016).

'The ICP network is of major importance to us', Kathrine Löfberg (personal communication, June 9, 2015) acknowledges. As Chairperson of the Board of International Coffee Partners, she maintains: 'With International Coffee Partners we enable long-term changes in the sector, and particularly for smallholder farming families. Sustainability efforts in our own supply chain is of course essential, but growing beyond single organizations and forming a sector-wide initiative shows our dedication and commitment to our vision: improving the livelihoods of coffee farming families worldwide in a long-term perspective' (*International Coffee Partners, About Us* 2016:1).

'Förpacknings- och Tidningsinsamlingen' (FTI; Packaging and Newspaper Collection Service) contributes to the building of a sustainable society. Since 1994, the Packaging Ordinance announces that 'all producers, i.e. companies which manufacture, import (from non-EU countries), bring in (from another EU member state) or sell packaging or packaged goods have a statutory responsibility for recovery of the packaging which placed onto the Swedish market' (*FTI's Instructions* 2015: 5). FTI is a nationwide recycling system for packaging, the role of which is to ensure that a collection system exists through which the customers and consumers of Löfbergs coffee can return used packaging and that collected packaging is recovered, recycled and put to good environmentally friendly use. Moreover, FTI makes sure that the customers and consumers are informed about the collection of used packaging. Approximately 10,000 companies affiliated with FTI are entitled to use the Green Dot symbol on their packaging, signalling that they meet the producer's requirements (*FTI* 2015).

In June 2015, the network Sustainable Food Chain was formed by large companies in the Swedish food industry. In addition to the Löfbergs Group, the network includes Arla, Axfood, Coop, Ica, Lantmännen, Orkla Foods Sverige, Polarbröd, HKScan, and Tetra Pak (*Hållbar Livsmedelskedja* 2016). 'The goal is to force the pace and increase the transition to a sustainable production and consumption of food through cooperation, dialogue and clear measures' (*Annual Report* 2014/2015: 16).

More local engagements in Karlstad encompass infrastructural investments; the building of a sports arena, shopping centre and congress facilities and the sponsoring of sport teams and associations. It should also be noted, in order to contribute to a greener urban environment locally, 100,000 'co-workers' have been hired. These are bees. 'In May, we hired 100,000 new co-workers in Karlstad. We are talking about bees living on our roof and contributing to a greener urban environment' (*Annual Report* 2013/2014: 33).

The networks present themselves as webs of distribution of ideas and collective actions that reach beyond group-related concerns and local places, characterizing the Löfbergs Group as a 'good social force'. This force translates into corporate and global citizenship through the exercise of different kinds of responsibilities.

Representing a Good Social Force

For the Löfbergs Group it is imperative to represent a 'good social force', engaging in a range of networks and projects both in the nearby environment and in the faraway coffee producing countries (*Annual Report* 2013/2014: 33). As Kathrine Löfberg (*Get to Know a Good Coffee* 2013: 4) asserts: 'As the world shrinks, we can get involved at the global level like never before – something we do more whole-heartedly than anyone else in the industry, I would say.' Network participation extends through webs of partners, defining both corporate and global citizenship. It mirrors engagement that ranges from nationwide recycling systems for packaging to worldwide projects, comprising a range of activities related to poverty reduction, anti-corruption activities, safety, health and education of children and women. By definition, corporate citizenship is 'the extent to which businesses meet the economic, legal, ethical, and discretionary responsibilities imposed on them by their stakeholders' (Hemphill 2004: 339). A global citizenship suggests involvement in supranational and intercultural dialogues, implying sensitivity to differences across cultures (Logsdon and Wood 2005). Based on such dialogues a mutual understanding can be achieved of how to approach and drive sustainable development (Hirsh Hadorn *et al.* 2006). In compliance with rules, affirmed by supranational laws, norms, standards, conventions and obligations and a national ordinance (as referred to in the preceding presentation of networks), the Löfbergs Group arguably broadens its scope, exercising global citizenship.

Through webs of partners, there is, in addition, the possibility for the group to generate competitive advantage. Following Elkington (1998: 50), 'companies with active, extended webs of partners will be much better prepared for emerging trends, their antenna scanning horizons well beyond the reach of many of their competitors.' The webs constitute structures that in support of the operations of the Löfbergs Group help to maintain competitiveness through being a good social force. This force relates to social capital, deriving from the partners' embedded relationships, the strengthening of relationships among the partners and their attendant responsibilities (Ayios *et al.* 2014). Social capital, defined as 'the goodwill that is endangered by the fabric of social relations and that can be mobilized to facilitate action' (Adler and Kwon 2002: 17), strongly influences collective action (Adger 2003). Yet, partner companies need to be reminded of the 'dark side' of social capital. While most approaches to social capital stress positive externalities such as trust and solidarity, negative externalities in the form of social exclusion (Ayios *et al.* 2014), echoes and structural holes (Ahuja 2000; Burt 1992) are downplayed. Social capital emanating from strong network ties could restrict the freedom of each partner and promote intolerance, leading to social exclusion of some partners. Echoes refer to a homogenization of perspectives that can occur over time when actors are closely interconnected. Echoes filter and sanitize information, which results in narrowing the network partners' views of sustainability work. Firms connected to other firms, not connected to each other, reside in structural holes. Such holes suggest weak connections between network partners and even empty spaces because partners have access to different flows of information. By participating in networks, the Löfbergs Group appears to share in and promote a good social force, the potency of which is realized through different kinds of responsibilities that help to maintain both corporate and global citizenship.

The group's participation in the networks seems to be predicated on the idea that CSR is an exercise of a broad range of responsibilities. A good social force must include social and environmental responsibilities along with economic ones; this is the core of the triple bottom line model (Elkington 1998). Although this model is difficult to apply to strategy practising mainly because of its lack of methodology for aggregating ethical performance into a single bottom line (Norman and Mac-Donald 2004), it nevertheless helps in elevating the ethical dimension of business life. The economic and ethical dimensions along with the legal and philanthropic add substance to the activities of CSR of the Löfbergs Group. Akin to the triple bottom line model, the social contract approach to CSR strikes a balance between profit making and social responsibilities as expressed in the duties and rights of corporations in society; planet, profit and people need to be aligned.

A good social force as represented by the Löfbergs Group can be discerned from the influence of the four responsibilities, economic, legal, ethical and philanthropic. These are summarized hierarchically by Carroll (1991: 42, emphasis in original) in the form of a pyramid: '*Be profitable. Obey the law. Be ethical. Be a good corporate citizen.*' Economic responsibilities provide the foundation of the pyramid upon which the legal, ethical and philanthropic responsibilities rest. As pointed out earlier, sustainability work performed by the Löfbergs Group is an integral part of the business model. 'Though profit making is not the purpose of business (from a societal perspective), it is essential as a motivation and reward for those individuals who take a commercial risk', clarifies

Carroll (2000: 35). Legal responsibilities reflect a view of codified ethics as established by law makers; in relation to the Löfbergs Group they are exemplified by the UN Sustainable Development Goals, EU obligations, norms and standards set by the Convention of the Rights of the Child, the Convention on the Elimination of All Forms of Discrimination against Women, and the Packaging Ordinance. Generally, following from the argument that corporations are legal units is that what a corporation does can be legitimately restricted. This actualizes a legal creator perspective according to which the corporation is obliged to contribute to the welfare of the society. 'The corporation as a privately hold good should, it is said, be used in a socially responsible way because it is also a public or common property, and therefore a common good' (Klonoski 1991: 14).

Ethical responsibilities implicate the stakeholder and the societal levels, embracing value and norms that society expects the organization to meet with a concern for what the stakeholder regards as fair and just. Acknowledged in the next section, a critical role of the Löfbergs Group management is to balance the demands articulated by the stakeholders and, at the same time, treat the stakeholders in an ethically responsible way. Philanthropic responsibilities, described as 'the icing of the cake', too concern good societal relations but in comparison with ethical responsibilities they are more discretionary in character. According to Hemphill (2004), although remaining anathema to proponents of shareholder wealth, strategic philanthropy (cf. Carroll 2000) has increasingly received management acceptance. It has become an integral part of a firm's strategy with 'a strong emphasis on employees' skill development and family support services, company moral building, and the enhancement of corporate social responsibility reputations' (Hemphill 2004: 341). In the case of the Löfbergs Group, philanthropic responsibilities appear to relate closely to global citizenship. The Löfbergs Group's participation in networks that support and promote the well-being of coffee farmers, children and women living in various parts of the world allows for a kind of philanthropy as something akin to global citizenship.

In order to expand the view of social responsibility, Wartick and Cochran (1985) updated Carroll's (1979) model. With reference to the corporate social performance (CSP) model they argued for a description of the totality of a firm's effort to meet changing social influences. This model, positively related to financial performance (Waddock and Graves 1997), retains a macro-level dimension through the use of social responsibility as a starting point for corporate social responsibility and includes a micro-level dimension through the focus on the interface between firm and environment. With its roots in general systems theory, the CSP model takes into consideration principles of social responsibility at the institutional, organizational and individual levels and accounts for processes of social responsiveness and outcomes (Wood 1991). In refining the CSP model, Kang and Wood (1995) flipped Carroll's (1979) model upside down, claiming that moral responsibility is the prime concern for all human organizations. Wood (2010: 55) concurs, taking the basic premise to be 'that no specific business organization has a right to survive if it cannot be profitable in legal and ethical ways; then social rightly will eliminate it.'

A stakeholder approach in combination with CSR indicates how managerial discretion is played out for the Löfbergs Group in association with strategic and multi-fiduciary intentions. The ethical obligation to be responsive to stakeholders is expressed as multi-fiduciary, which requires considerations beyond profit maximization (Jamali 2008). Principles of social responsibility are articulated, and processes and outcomes are taken into account by the group. In accordance with the CSP model, this makes us aware of the institutional level.

Without Discriminating between Stockholder and Stakeholder
According to Goodpaster (1991), the relationship between management and stockholders is ethically different in kind from the relationship between management and other stakeholders because the management could have both a strategic and multi-fiduciary intention. The strategic intention of management is generally to keep a profit maximizing promise to the stockholders, whereas the fiduciary intention is to fulfil an ethical obligation associated with care and loyalty to the stakeholders. The inherent paradox holds that managers who 'pursue a multi-fiduciary stakeholder orientation for their companies must face resistance from those who believe that a strategic orientation is the only *legitimate* one for business to adopt, given the economic mission and legal constitution of the modern corporation' (Goodpaster 1991: 63, emphasis in original). Without discriminating between stockholder and stakeholder, the management of the Löfbergs Group handles this paradox by pursuing a multi-fiduciary orientation entwined with the strategic intention to achieve long-term profitable growth. The management indicates that sustainability work includes 'investing in the right areas, which in turn leads to innovation, efficient resource utilisation and good relation with our stakeholders' (*Sustainability Report* 2012/2013: 11). The stakeholders are owners, board of directors, employees, suppliers, customers, consumers and society (*Annual Report* 2014/2015). A critical role for the management is to balance the competing demands of the stakeholders (Harrison and Freeman 1999) and treat

them in a socially responsible way. Enduring and socially responsible ties with all stakeholders are of strategic importance to the management of the Löfbergs Group, the moral claim of which is inherent in sustainability work and accentuated by ethical indicators, policies, codes of conduct and ISO standards.

The sustainability work is evaluated and reported regularly in the sustainability report, included in the annual report. It complies with the international ethical guidelines of the Global Reporting Initiative (GRI) for generating reliable and standardized information about sustainability impacts. Compiled and estimated by external parties, the sustainability report accounts for areas such as the group's strategy, profile, work environment and relationships with the stakeholders. The report builds on financial, environmental and industry-specific indicators (*Annual Report* 2013/2014).

Policies for quality and food safety, sustainability, work environment, personnel and purchasing do all emphasize the maintenance of 'the right quality' and 'good ethics' in decisions and in communication with the stakeholders, ensuring that Löfbergs as a group is an ethical producer of coffee (*Coffee Group Document* 2012–2016). The Code of Conduct and the business ethics policy further urge the companies of the group to act socially responsible in all operations with the stakeholders while striving for continuous improvements. The Code of Conduct originates in the United Nation (UN) and the International Labour Organization (ILO) regulations and conventions for human rights, stipulating requirements for supplying 'top-quality' products produced in a sustainable manner (*Code of Conduct* 2015). The business ethics policy provides guidance for the daily work, covering areas such as bribery and corruption, gifts, meals and entertainment, donations, competition law and financial irregularities (*Business Ethics Policy* 2014).

In case of a behavioural misfit with current policies and the Code of Conduct, the employee as internal stakeholder is urged to report to the immediate manager or another representative in the company management. The system for confidential reporting via the Intranet could be used if the employee would prefer to keep his or her identity secret (*Business Ethics Policy* 2014). Through whistle-blowing, unethical organizational behaviors can be disclosed. Eva Eriksson (personal communication, February 13, 2015) explains:

So far, none has felt the urge to blow the whistle installed on the website on our Intranet. We have informed everyone that it is there and we have performed tests to ensure that it works. So when you see something you believe violates or ignores the principles set by our business ethics policy, the whistleblower function can be used to communicate anonymously that situation.

'Whistleblowing is a form of self-diagnosis and can be effective to prevent a minor wrongdoing from developing into a crisis' (Chen and Lai 2014: 327). But an individual's loyalty to the organization may blind his or her perception of wrongdoing. In addition, as sustainability activities become more complex and less visible it could be difficult to detect inappropriate actions, and whistle-blowing might even produce harm and retaliation, as Chen and Lai (2014) add. From a whistle-blowing perspective the receiver is important and the effectiveness of whistle-blowing depends on how the receiver scans the environment for signals, attunes to looking for the signal, acts on it and provides feedback to the signaller (Janney and Folta 2006).

In communication with the stakeholders, without discriminating between stockholder and stakeholder, the Löfbergs Group allegedly strengthens the corporate and global citizenships, adherence with which is a good social force. To maintain these citizenships ISO standards are also implemented. ISO 9001 concerns quality management systems, ISO 14001 environmental management systems and ISO 22000 management systems for food safety (*Annual Report* 2013/2014). Corporations tend to adopt these standards to legitimize their operations, through written, distinct and formal documents (Schwartz 2005) setting out and communicating practices expected of the employees at all levels in the organization (Webley and Werner 2008) and other stakeholders. Legitimization introduces agency with reference to the institutional level; coloured in green it accounts for sustainability.

Joining the 'Green' Organization Theorists

Especially 'green' organization theorists underline the usefulness of institutional theory as an approach to sustainable organization. Joining the green theorists, Jennings and Zandbergen (1995: 1016) contend that institutional theory helps us to understand how practices associated with sustainability 'come to have a "rule-like, social fact quality" and how they become "embedded" in institutions and organizational fields.' Through the Löfbergs Group's documentation, application and spread of rules, conferred and attempted by ethical guidelines through policies, the Code of Conduct and ISO standards, and through the application of supranational rules, the allocation and use of resources as prescribed by the networks partners, CSR is established as an institutionalized feature. As Brammer, Jackson and Matten (2012: 10) acknowledge, 'CSR has even become a strong institutionalized feature of the contemporary corporate landscape in advanced industrial economies ... The institutionalization of CSR can be seen in the diffusion of CSR departments within companies, the spread of stock market indices related to sustainability, the proliferation of branding institutions and even an ISO standard of CSR.'

Arguably, institutionalization of CSR legitimizes the Löfbergs Group's sustainability work. Embedded in economic, legal, ethical and philanthropic responsibilities (Carroll 1991, 2000), the sustainability work, normatively sanctioned by the network partners and other stakeholders, promotes the development of a 'good social force' in conjunction with corporate and global citizenships. In accordance with Wood's (1991) version of the corporate social performance model, the CSR practising of the Löfbergs Group also accounts for processes and outcomes through which ethical areas and indicators promulgated by international GRI guidelines are identified, evaluated and reported. In the legitimization of sustainability work, we note a reconciliation of the 'what' explained by Carroll's (1991, 2000) model and the 'how' by Wood's (1991, 2010) model.

Institutional theory built around sustainability also focuses on how consensus about the meaning of sustainability is developed and diffused among organizations for legitimizing sustainability work (Brammer, Jackson and Matten 2012; Verbeke and Tung 2013). But when exposed to multiple institutional contexts there is potential for structural change, accomplished through improvization, experimentation and rejection of rules (Delbridge and Edwards 2013; Johnson, Smith and Codling 2010; Whittington 2015). However, as a result of the rather limited and cursory discussion in this chapter, there are no indications of contradictions and tensions within and across the presented networks in which the Löfbergs Group participates or attempts to outmanoeuvre partners and undermine the network structure. Neither are there indications of contestation over meanings of CSR among the network partners and the other stakeholders, or difficulties on the part of the group management in coordinating and balancing the stakeholders' varying goals and demands. Yet, we should be aware that there could be political struggles when trying to shape, align and homogenize interests among stakeholders for legitimizing sustainability work. There might be situations where a 'P', standing for political issues, must be added to CSR.

Increased demands from stakeholders placed on the Löfbergs Group might cause political activity, altering the bargaining positions of some stakeholders. As indicated by the owner and Purchasing Director Martin Löfberg (*Code of Conduct* 2015: 1): 'Interested stakeholders (customers, consumers, Non-Governmental Organisations, etc.) are to an increasing extent placing demands on our company and products in terms of our responsibility to the society in which we work, i.e. Corporate Social

Responsibility (CSR).' Sustainability Director Eva Eriksson (personal communication, February 13, 2015) even directly uses the term 'political': 'Sustainability work includes a political game. Within the network of the Haga initiative, we are currently in the process of developing a document, the so-called position paper, to be presented at the Ministry of Industry in Stockholm before the Environmental Advisory Council. So we also engage in the establishment of policies and regulatory frameworks.'

Political corporate social responsibility (PSCR) allows for sustainability to be reconstituted over time through struggles and game playing in interactions between non-governmental organizations (NGOs) and coffee companies. This has implications for green institutionalized practising. Although multi-national coffee roasters adapt the discourse of sustainability in discussion with their stakeholders it seems that this can be done mainly for rhetorical reasons for managing reputation and promoting market-oriented goals. NGO standards adapted to suit mainstream business models, incorporating productivity measures into sustainability, have transformed the meaning of sustainability 'from a more radical environmental and social vision to a set of management processes that aligned with corporate goals', Levy, Reinecke and Manning (2016: 390) remark. CSR has gained a political character. It should be acknowledged, though, that the International Safety Equipment Association (ISEA), formed in 2002 by NGOs, serves as gatekeeper to distinguish credible claims from misleading ones (Levy, Reinecke and Manning 2016).

In accordance with CEO Lars Appelqvist it is important to integrate sustainability work into the business model because it strengthens the brand and decreases costs (*Annual Report* 2013/2014). Sustainability reduces the carbon footprint and generates competitive advantage for the firm in its specific industry, ecosystem and neighbourhood, adds McPhee (2014). Thus, there might not be a substantial clash between sustainability and business performance. It seems impossible to reduce sustainability to a discourse for reputation and market-oriented goals since CSR in combination with a stakeholder approach is not imposed from the outside of the Löfbergs Group but continuously incorporated. Indeed, from the beginning of the last century, the Löfberg family has been importing and selling coffee, using principles associated with CSR as a natural and important part of their operations (Kathrine Löfberg, *Get to Know a Good Coffee* 2013). Also with regard to the multiplicity of initiatives, addressed and implemented by the networks in which the group actively participates, we acknowledge the application of a broader sustainability discourse. The CSR principles, documented, applied and spread through an array of national and supranational rules, provide legitimacy to the sustainability work of the Löfbergs Group. In ascribing moral agency to this coffee group, we account for a 'green' institutional level, but to gain more insight into moral agency we need to move beyond that level.

Moving beyond the Group Level

Notwithstanding the importance of looking into the coffee context defined by the group organization with its strong focus on morality in association with sustainability and CSR, it is pertinent to note that more light needs to be shed on moral agency as expressed and effectuated in activities with which Löfbergs-practitioners and other humans entwine. An organization is no super person or moral agent able to take action in the name of sustainability and CSR. 'Organization' cannot be kicked, whipped or imprisoned (Danley 1980). Consistent with the idea introduced by Roman law 'of the corporate body, the *universitas*, as a juristic person, albeit a fictional one' (Coleman 1990: 533, emphasis in original), organization in the form of a corporation is detached from the individual and, accordingly, individual responsibility from corporate responsibility. We should therefore critically reflect on the basis on which organization is attributed personhood and depicted as an agent 'morally culpable in a way either identical with or very similar to natural persons' (Klonoski 1991: 10).

A coffee context predefined by the Löfbergs Group and conceived of as an empirical unit is subjected to an understanding that operates in favour of ontic concerns, where ontic implies a description of what already exists with a focus on cause–effect relationships (Stefanovic 2000). This assumes a representational view of the world (Helin *et al.* 2014). Under the supposition that there is no unit that corresponds to a thing obtained directly from experience ready to study, one becomes aware that it is important to distinguish between a word and a thing, and the meaning of a word and a thing (Wells 1993). There is no entity in the form of an organization, whether labelled system, collective, corporation, firm, company or group, owing its supposed existence to the concept of substance.

From a relational-ontological horizon the presentation of the group context mounts a springboard (Chapter 1) that provides impetus for opening a window to an empirical-theoretical discussion that appreciates human betweenness. As purported by Helin *et al.* (2014: 13): 'Studying the world relationally acknowledges the performative nature of research. Research, in the non-representational sense, does not leave the world alone when describing and modelling it. It takes part as we imagine relationships and "explanations" without regulating origins or objectives anchored as touchstones of truth.' When going beyond the group level we encounter 'context' as space that comes into being and forms through human in-betweens, as Chapter 5 illustrates.

5 'Our Good Will'
An Emerging Coffee Context

'Coffee is artwork ... coffee is conscientiously grown, the small plant is carefully attended and cultivated to produce cherries ... lots of people are involved in picking, sorting, grading, drying, transporting and processing the coffee cherries ... you need to take productivity, sustainability, ethical and social aspects into account', highlights Charlotta Stenson, Business Development Manager (personal communication, October 28, 2011).

The artwork of coffee most likely has its origins in Ethiopia. The word 'coffee' sounds similar to 'Kaffe', the name of a region in Ethiopia. According to Sinnott (2010), the legend tells that coffee was discovered by the goat herder Kaldi, who observed that one of his goats chewed on some cherries and began dancing. The herder tasted these cherries and also experienced an energized feeling. He took some cherries to the local monastery for closer scrutinizing. The monks roasted the cherries in the fire and coffee was created.

With reference to Löfbergs coffee, the art and work of coffee can be described by the from-bean-to-cup chain, encompassing growing, transportation, processing, distribution and consumption activities with which practitioners, associated with the Löfbergs Group (Löfbergs-practitioners), coffee farmers, representatives of development and certification projects, customers and consumers entwine. Applying Ricoeur's (1992) concept of practice, there is a long chain of activities, coordinated causally and intentionally. The activities are linearly planned through a means–ends model. Coffee assigned the Löfbergs label also suggests non-linearity, exposed through people's entwinement with and variable connections to a present and a past. Practising performed at present reactivates a past while orienting towards a future.

To convey a temporal-relational sense of what is entailed by moral human agency we need to include 'good'. According to Taylor (1989) you cannot get a clear picture of human agency without an understanding of the good. Löfbergs-practitioners in interaction with other people pronounce and activate a good will, fundamentally anchored in the five

67

values: responsibility, commitment, long-term approach, entrepreneurship and professionalism (referred to as good-will values). In dialogical openness to the Other, Löfbergs coffee thus furnishes a reference point that broadens our horizon of strategy practising, in this chapter affording an interpretation and understanding that account for both linearity and non-linearity in the constitution of 'our-good-will' context. As Löfbergspractitioners articulate and effectuate the good-will values interactively with others the coffee context emerges. Through 'good-willed' practising, moral human agency unfolds the projective, practical-evaluative and iterational dimensions. The projective dimension reveals itself through present value chain activities with which Löfbergs-practitioners and others entwine when imagining and creating a sustainable future. The practical-evaluative dimension too serves as a point of reference for an interpretation and understanding of moral human agency in future-oriented practising but includes, in addition, normative judgement that implies a reconsideration of past ways of engaging in value chain activities. The iterational dimension addresses a past that is currently called on and reactivated by the practitioners. As the antithesis of objectivity, our-good-will context refers to a world of practising to which the practitioners belong as social-historical beings.

The chapter is structured in three sections. The first two sections direct attention to value chain activities. The third section focuses on a value-laden past and a 'purple' intention. A commentary rounds off each section, pointing to the temporal-relational character of moral human agency.

Good-Willed Growing, Transportation and Processing

The term 'good-willed' is used in connection with practising that comprises growing, transportation and processing activities, permeated by values. Five values, referred to as good-will values, are articulated by Löfbergs-practitioners and actualized in their activities. CEO Lars Appelqvist (personal communication, August 31, 2015) explains: 'Our good will is exercised though the five values, responsibility, commitment, long-term approach, entrepreneurship and professionalism, interwoven with financial considerations that help strengthening competitiveness.' 'The values have been made alive throughout our whole history, reminding us of the founding owners. The values have become even more accentuated over the past years and we also use them as tools in our daily activities', adds Kathrine Löfberg, owner, Chairman of the Board of Directors (personal communication, June 9, 2015).

Five Löfbergs-practitioners, four of whom represent subsidiaries in the United Kingdom, Latvia, Norway and Denmark (*Sustainability Report* 2012/2013: 23), further explain what the values mean. We note that 'responsibility' is used in close association with commitment, genuine engagement and respect. Heather Lawrence, United Kingdom: 'Assuming responsibility for the environment and the world around us is a given. At the same time it's all about respect for colleagues and customers, to make everything work.' Maija Pētersone, Latvia: 'Genuine engagement creates pride, it contributes to improving the quality of our work and of our products, and to our enjoying tremendous trust among our customers.' Mette Nyegaard Serkland, Norway: 'We work with an exciting product that engages lots of people. We have to constantly be innovative and learn new things in order to keep up.' Micheal Elkjaer, Denmark: 'By helping one another to always keep our promises, we create sustainable, long-term relations, internally and with our customers.' Zeljko Cordasic, Sweden: 'For me, professionalism means doing your best at all times – for customers, the company and its employees. And that's the way I think it is with us.' Niklas Löfberg (*Annual Report* 2013/2014: 7), owner, summarizes: 'Taking responsibility for people and the environment has always been important for us as owners. For us, it is a prerequisite for a long-term, sustainable and profitable business.'

In among Löfbergs-Practitioners, Coffee Farmers and ICP Representatives

Coffee beans are purchased from farmers in South America, Central America, East Africa and Asia (Chapter 4). The major part is from South America (*Annual Report* 2014/2015). 'We buy directly from about 40,000 farmers who constitute what we call first-commercial entry point', says Lars Appelqvist (personal communication, March 31, 2014). Owner and Purchasing Director Martin Löfberg highlights: 'We never compromise on the great flavour. We purchase all coffee straight from the producing country and have long-term and close relationships with coffee farmers to guarantee the high quality' (*Fair and Good* 2013: 5). All coffee originates from the *Coffea arabica* plant species. As Sinnott (2010: 36, emphasis in original) clarifies: 'Several coffee plant-species fall under the Rubiaceae family, genus name *Coffea*. Arabica is the original cultivated plant species and the one that offers the finest potential flavour.' Direct purchasing meets high requirements for traceability, demonstrating how the value of responsibility instrumentally applies and what the implications are for the whole value chain. Kathrine Löfberg (personal communication, June 9, 2015), clarifies: 'Taking responsibility for traceability is essential in our view. In order to fulfil our requirements on traceability we purchase coffee directly from the producing countries. It is imperative for us to exercise control over coffee production, building a transparent chain from growing to consumption.' The farmers are organized into small family businesses and cooperatives. A cooperative is owned by its members, who, following the democratic principle of one member one vote, have a say in matters concerning the cooperative (Pestoff 1991). The members contribute capital to their cooperative in an equitable manner, investing in a membership share.

Two Löfbergs-practitioners, the present Purchasing Director Martin Löfberg and the senior Trading Manager Tony Broman, spend about 150 days per year visiting the plantations. They work in close spatial proximity with the farmers, generating and exchanging information and ideas for future planning. In interaction with representatives of International Coffee Partners (ICP; Chapter 4) they implement and follow up on improvements concerning, for instance, the use of more advanced technical equipment beneficial to the coffee farmers' working and living environment, better transportation means, the possibility to produce larger volumes at lower costs for raising the income and reducing dependence on intermediaries. In among the Löfbergs-practitioners, coffee farmers and ICP representatives ample opportunity for learning about each other's challenges is provided. In a projective and practical-evaluative sense, these in-betweens contribute changes for meeting high-quality demands at present and in the future.

Closely associated with raised requirements of sustainable production is reciprocity. The in-betweens reflect ooperation among the Löfbergs-practitioners, the coffee farmers and the ICP representatives, affording reciprocity in terms of mutual benefit and respect. Appelqvist comments (personal communication, March 31, 2014):

We feel that we can do well in the long term in our relations with the coffee farmers, who are totally dependent on revenues from coffee production for their survival. The value of long-term is important also for our owners, who wish to keep the business alive and thriving in the 2050s, the point in time at which the next generation is supposed to take over. Then there must be a truly sustainable coffee production and especially in the producing countries it is crucial to reflect on how we behave. In cooperation with the coffee farmers we must create conditions for a long-term sustainable coffee production and generate benefits to their community as a whole. So this cooperation really matters to us.

It is important to consider, according to the CEO, that 'the growing of coffee is where the single biggest element of our climate impact exists (*Sustainability Report* 2102/2013: 4). More than 80 per cent of the impact of carbon dioxide takes place at the growing stage (*Annual Report* 2012/2013).

On a Trip to Honduras and Other Places On a trip to Honduras, Martin Löfberg visited a number of coffee farmers organized as cooperatives. Often through difficult terrain he travels on foot. The cooperative Café Orgánico Marcla (COMSA) in Honduras consists of eight hundred small-scale farmers who organically grow arabica at an altitude of 1,200-1,700 metres (*Annual Report* 2014/2015). Löfberg (personal communication, May 18, 2015) engages in the establishment of cooperatives, making sure that they meet basic eligibility criteria for certification. Responsible for operational controls of Fairtrade and EU organic coffee, he also is involved in certification activities and follow-ups of the cooperatives' work. Fairtrade certification concerns the coffee farmers' working and living conditions, guaranteeing the farmer a minimum price for coffee and the cooperative an extra premium. If assigned the EU Organic label, the producer assuredly complies with the EU regulation for organic production (*Annual Report* 2014/2015). Thomas Andersson, Sales Director (personal communication, February 25, 2015), remarks:

Fairtrade is the only certification where the farmer is guaranteed a minimum price, which is higher and includes a floor price compared to the trading price determined by the Stock Exchange. Fairtrade enjoys an exclusive position among certifications. Nearly all Fairtrade-coffee plantations are run by families that contribute small crops and therefore, they are strongly dependent on coffee. It is their only source of income and when getting well paid they are able to improve their living conditions, and among other things, also provide opportunities for their children's education.

Moreover, ethical certification includes Krav, Rainforest Alliance, and UTZ Certified. Krav promises that no chemical pesticides, artificial fertilizers and genetically modified organisms are used in the production. Rainforest Alliance signifies biodiversity and farmers' sustainable livelihood, and the UTZ Certified label too focuses on the living standard by prompting improvements in productivity, product quality and efficiency (*Annual Report* 2013/2014).

Martin Löfberg (personal communication, May 18, 2015) describes the establishment of a cooperative, its certification and ongoing existence:

The first step is to decide who qualify as members of the cooperative and discuss the advantages of working together as a cooperative and then, linking together and integrating the members' competencies. When a cooperative has been established and certified it is immediately exposed to a faked trading situation. We pretend to buy a container of raw coffee. The exchanges between the buyer and the seller, product and money, provide important learning potential. Qualified as traders, the coffee farmers are capable of running a business as a cooperative. Through calibrating the quality of coffee, maintaining sustainability, the cooperative is assured continued existence. Today, raw coffee is purchased from more than 40 cooperatives.

Lars Appelqvist (personal communication, March 31, 2014) interjects: 'We prefer to do business with a cooperative. It denotes an appropriate level of aggregation, considering our annual production of coffee based on approximately 600,000 bags. An individual farmer produces about 40 bags per year.'

Martin Löfberg (personal communication, May 18, 2015) continues:

So, the cooperative ventures often begin by offering the farmers the opportunity to deliver one or two containers to us. Getting started with the coffee trade is a key. We wish to have strong partners, commercially capable to supply quality and deliver on time at a price agreed on. Purchasing criteria, generally applicable to any coffee provider with a commercial interest, must be met. The cooperatives are investing in hard work to become certified and it is a long process that requires lots of resources. Purchasing criteria are supplemented by social criteria specified by the certification. This means, for example, that certain managerial abilities must be developed and improvement has to be made in infrastructure. In remote and desolate locations where heavy rains wash the roads away, farmers are faced with major infrastructural challenges. We want the coffee growers to be empowered to operate on a long-term basis to improve their productivity and livelihood, the main source of which is coffee.

In El Salvador, Tanzania, Kenya, India, Peru, Vietnam and Brazil, for example, Löfbergs-practitioners run development projects together with coffee farmers and their families in support of ICP representatives (*Annual Report* 2014/2015; *International Coffee Partners* 2016). Since 2001, a large number of ICP projects have been implemented. In 2013, eighteen projects were initiated and completed, directly involving twenty thousand coffee farmers (*We Work for the Coffee Growers for the Environment 2014*). Appelqvist (personal communication, August 31, 2015) reveals:

Some of these projects are co-financed by the Bill Gates Foundation and SIDA. The projects encourage coffee farmers to learn about economic and financial conditions, understanding how the market works and how their working methods affect product quality, price and income. They learn about climate change and the importance of not using too much pesticide. We are also concerned about infrastructure in areas such as roads and health care. After three years have passed we dismantle the project and in conjunction with that we ensure that a local organization continues the work in accordance with the guidelines of the project. A project cannot be abruptly shut down; it must remain in existence, preparing the next step for fulfilling specific requirements and certification criteria.

With a special focus on climate, Löfbergs-practitioners, together with representatives of SIDA (Sweden) and GIZ (Germany), work with the

Coffee & Climate project, developing a tool box to be used by coffee farmers for improving the possibility to cope with climate changes (*Annual Report* 2014/2015). The farmer Maurico Gavarrete, Tanzania (*Projects Tanzania, International Coffee Partner* 2016: 1), shares his experience with the project: 'In my region, the most hitting consequences of climate changes are the rising temperature and drought. With the support of Coffee & Climate, we started experimenting the distance we plant our trees in, and have re-invented our traditional way of farming coffee by introducing cover crops and gypsum.' A cover crop is a plant grown to manage soil erosion and control diseases (*Definition Cover Crop Small Farms* 2016). Gypsum is a natural sulphate mineral used for changing the structure of soil (Grant 2015).

A few other examples of projects conducted in interactions of Löfbergs-practitioner, coffee farmers and ICP representatives, include the cooperative Othaya in Kenya for Fairtrade approval, a large farm in India in conversion to Rainforest Alliance and the establishment of a water energy station in Peru. As witnessed by Don Fredrico, coffee farmer in the Amazon district, Peru: 'Through hard work as well as the organic and Fairtrade certifications of my farm, I have increased my crops, the quality and my incomes. That makes my family and I manage better. I hope it will make it easier to pass the farm on to my children' (*Annual Report* 2013/2014: 19).

Mr Oanh, coffee farmer in the district of Di Linh, Vietnam, too refers to the benefits of being involved in an ICP project. Tony Broman, who from a great many years of experience travelling the coffee-producing world has been given the epithet 'Löfbergs Indiana Jones', met with Mr Oanh. Acting at a meeting at the Ministry of Agriculture in Hanoi as a spokesperson for other coffee growers in Di Linh, Mr Oanh, declared: 'Thanks to the ICP project, my colleagues and I in the district have learned a great deal about better coffee growing methods. I have also gained extra knowledge by taking part in courses for new instructors. I now feel much more confident about training other growers or talking to a group of people' (*We Work for the Coffee Growers for the Environment* 2014: 7).

Further, through ICP project activities, technical guidance is made accessible for coffee farmers in the south-east of Brazil. One of the farmers is Sr. Jesus. Although his production of coffee beans has always been of a good quality there is room for improvement on production practices and on bean quality that will help reduce production costs. The increased harvest, from an average of 28 coffee bags per year to 52 bags in 2015, has yielded positive income. Always accompanying the agricultural engineers during their visits to the farm, Sr. Jesus has learned to apply their guidelines for control of pests and diseases. By conducting soil and leaf analysis he is able to make an appropriate choice and dose of fertilizer. Notably, more advanced knowledge about production practices and classification of quality has strengthened his bargaining position in relation to local brokers. On a less positive note is that the son of Sr. Jesus recently left the family plantation to work in one of the bigger cities. Yet the Brazilian coffee farmer's dream is to expand the plantation by planting two thousand new coffee trees. He hopes to enable his son to move back and to see his grandchildren grow up (*Projects Brazil, 2015; International Coffee Partners* 2016).

Close cooperation with the growers 'makes it easier for us to work with social and environmental responsibility, but also allows us to pay well and provides us with useful feedback for the future. Does our involvement make a difference? Absolutely! I see it first-hand on my travels', Tony Broman highlights (Löfberg 2013: 7). Martin Löfberg (*Annual Report* 2013/2014: 19) too refers to advantages of interacting with the coffee farmers face-to-face: 'On my trips, I can see with my own eyes that sustainable farming methods have positive effects for the coffee farmer and the local community. It feels great to be able to contribute to that.'

The so-called Eco Receipt (included in *Annual Report* 2014/2015) reveals what close and long-term relationships between coffee farmers and Löfbergs-practitioners produce in terms of sustainable production. In 2014, a land area of the size of approximately twelve thousand football arenas was converted to sustainable production, and the use of artificial fertilizers and chemical pesticides substantially decreased. Besides, by purchasing Fairtrade-certified coffee from farmers organized as cooperatives, Löfbergs-practitioners contributed to a premium of approximately MSEK 16 and an increase in revenues exceeding MSK 24 for the cooperatives in the financial year of 2013/2014 (*Annual Report* 2013/2014).

At the Final Destination in Karlstad Streamlined train transportation and smart packaging considerably lower the number of transports and the amount of emissions of carbon dioxide. On a yearly basis estimated savings of carbon dioxide corresponds to the emissions of 1,540 flights between Stockholm and New York (*Annual Report* 2013/2014). 'The coffee beans travel a long way - from countries such as Colombia, Brazil, Kenya and Ethiopia, packed in a large bulk of 21 tons, sealed in a big bag placed in a container or packed in jute sacks of 60 or 70 kilos in a container or stacked on pallets', reports Johan Eriksson, Process Operator and Club Chairman of the Swedish Food Workers' Union (personal communication, November 13, 2015). Reloaded onto trains, the main share continues to the Löfbergs roasting house in Karlstad. A smaller share is taken to Viborg in Denmark and Riga in Latvia for further transport by truck to the roasting houses. At the final destination in Karlstad the processing starts with inspection of the coffee beans and continues through roasting and taste testing.

At the interim storage facilities in Brazil one has prepared a sample of small bags of raw coffee to be directly removed from the container and tested on arrival in Karlstad. When approved and stored, each type of coffee beans is processed in a silo and before roasting, cleaning is done for eliminating residue of rocks and dust, ensuring that different coffee bean types are not mixed in the silo. The processing is based on customer orders that can vary from 1 tons to 30-40 tons. On the basis of the order, careful planning is done and the order is batched into units appropriated for roasting (Johan Eriksson personal communication, November 13, 2015).

The processing takes place in the Löfbergs Scraper, reaching forty-seven metres into the sky, accessible to the public for guided tours. Receptionist and Tour Guide Marlene Högefjord (personal communication, June 12, 2016) tells:

During 2015, there were about 300 visitors. Over the past few years, the number of visitors has steadily increased. The visitors show an interest in the processing of coffee and in the ecological aspect and some are looking for a job opportunity in Löfbergs. Most surprising to them is that a great many beans are required for processing a cup of coffee and that coffee production, from converting the raw bean into the finished coffee, is such a long and complex process.

Roasting converts raw green coffee beans to a state called parolysis, which, occurring at the elevated temperature of around 210 degrees Celsius, changes the organic composition of substances. This suggests a moment of truth – a moment at which roasting makes the taste of coffee known (Sinnott 2010). In preparation for this moment, Johan Eriksson (personal communication, November 13, 2015) presses the button for heating the roasting machine:

At around 5.30 in the morning I press the button for heating the roasting machine, which consists of a horizontal rotating drum for preheating the coffee at 80 degree Celsius, and for the actual roasting, a stainless bowl that looks like a wok pan 2.5 meter in diameter. After approximately 40 minutes the entire bowl is hot and you can put the right batch size of raw coffee into the bowl. The roasting is processed according to a recipe that each customer order, assigned an article number, specifies. The recipe also defines the grinding grade, which varies depending on the customer's preference for boiled or brewed coffee. Upon completing the roasting, the coffee is degassed for about three hours. Conditional on the roasting temperature, water might evaporate, emerging as white smoke from the chimney on the roof of our Scraper.

Green electricity from wind power is used for roasting, geothermal heating for heating coffee, and district heating for the heating of the roasting facility. The world's first large-scale testing facility of solar panels has been built for heating and cooling. In order to decrease carbon dioxide emissions further, improvements have been made to insulation of pipes in one roasting machine. Technical Manager Jan Möttönen (*Annual Report* 2014/2015: 25) comments:

Our use of electricity is as low as it was in the beginning of the 1990s while the coffee production has doubled! The greatest improvement was when we introduced preheating of the green coffee beans by recycling the hot air from the roasting, a technique we were first in Europe with and that decreased the energy use with 20 per cent.

Grinding, packing and loading are activities that linearly follow on the processing activities. Johan Eriksson (personal communication, September 4, 2015) describes the process:

Before the customer receives the coffee we check carefully for quality in terms of right texture, colour, taste ... Every day we send samples of coffee to our laboratory technicians for testing. Yes, quality first and foremost. What we do, must be right. We must roast and grind right so the end product satisfies the customer's taste, making sure that our high quality standards are met.

The taste is evaluated through coffee cupping, described by Sinnott (2010: 47) as 'the stop-and-smell-the-roses step in your development as a coffee drinker.' 'Flower' is among the 899 tastes contained in one cup of Löfbergs coffee (*Kafferosteriet Löfbergs* 2016). Anna Nordström (personal communication, August 4, 2015), Specialty Coffee Manager, underlines the importance of distinguishing between aroma and taste:

These two features of coffee are relatively easily conflated. When we refer to taste we should be aware that we often describe aroma. In order to separate the two you hold your nose; what you sense when holding your nose is the taste and when releasing the grip on the nose, the aroma emerges. Löfbergs coffee defines a rich array of aromas, which are highly dependent on the water quality and the methods and equipment you use for processing coffee.

Unfolding Moral Human Agency – Commentary (I)

As indicated in this section, good-willed practising, constituted of growing, transportation and processing activities, unfolds moral human agency in the projective and practical-evaluative dimensions. The projective dimension accentuates the generation of new ideas translated to future practising. Through the Löfbergs-practitioners' use of the good-will values (responsibility, commitment, long-term approach, entrepreneurship and professionalism) as tools for developing and improving qualities related to growing, transportation and processing of coffee beans, the practical-evaluative dimension is actualized. When faced with raised demands on quality these tools provide a basis for the practitioners' practical normative judgements. Cooperation, exchange of information and learning among Löfbergs-practitioners, coffee farmers and ICP representatives entail in-betweens that engage the practical-evaluative dimension, proposing a move in a future direction that deviates from a past. Cooperation fosters openness to the Other and a cross-fertilization of ideas that reconciles cultural differences (Katz and Martin 1997). Cooperation facilitates learning among responsible and committed people. Social in character (e.g. Fichtner 1999; Dreier 2003; Suchman and Trigg 2003), promoted through human in-betweens (McDermott 2003) and not limited to individual (Lave 2003), learning suggests being in relation to the Other (Todd 2003).

As illustrated, interactions of Martin Löfberg, Tony Broman, coffee farmers and ICP representatives mainly engage a practical-evaluative dimension of moral human agency. Agreeing on mutual justifiable and fair principles as specified by certification and ICP development projects in integration with laws and regulations that prevail in the coffee-producing countries, they involve making practical normative judgements for promoting sustainable growing. The practical-evaluative dimension elicits a moral human agency that in its present–future orientation prompts a temporal reorientation through distancing a past characterized by unarticulated concerns for sustainability. In interactions of Löfbergs-practitioners, coffee farmers and ICP representatives past-oriented routines for growing are adjusted and recomposed in order to increase the farmers' income and decrease their use of chemical pesticides and artificial fertilizers.

It is, in addition, worth noting that good will appears to be expressed in interactions among the coffee farmers and the members of their families. From the viewpoint of the Peruvian farmer Don Fredrico, good will extends the hope that his children will continue growing coffee trees. The Brazilian farmer Sr. Jesus gives voice to a more pessimistic outlook because his son is leaving the family plantation for work in one of the bigger cities. Yet, a good will seems to be enveloped in a tacit hope that the son will move back.

Further, it is indicated that material plays a role in the growing, transportation and processing of coffee beans; as exemplified in relation to growing: geographical place, rain, drought, soil and physical tools the farmers utilize; in relation to transportation: road, vehicle and fuel; in relation to processing: isolation pipe, roasting machine, customer recipe and 'green' electricity. Materials help to extend human agency

(Sandberg and Dall'Alba 2009; Tsoukas 2015), constituting human–non-human betweenness. Future-oriented concerns pronounced with respect to human and non-human in-betweens give relief to the project-ive dimension, and insofar as cooperation is fostered in altered ways through the utilization of new material, the practical-evaluative dimension is made salient. But when everything runs smoothly through the value chain, it can be assumed in agreement with Tsoukas (2015) that practitioners immerse themselves in unanticipated and unplanned activities that transpire within existing material arrangements.

Good-Willed Distribution and Consumption

The term 'good-willed' is also applicable to the practising of distribution and consumption. The good-will values serve as guides for distribution and consumption, constituting a moral human agency characterized as projective and practical-evaluative. The practising suggests in-betweens among Löfbergs-practitioners, customers, consumers and competitors through which different kinds of challenges are managed.

Löfbergs-practitioners, interacting under the department labels of 'Retail' and 'Out of Home', answer for the main part of distribution of coffee. Retail, the trade of convenience goods includes big customers such as the ICA Group, Coop and Axfood, who have consolidated their positions as leading players in the Swedish retail market, reports Sales Director Kent Pettersson (personal communication, February 3, 2015). Out of Home serves customers such as Nordic Choice, Scandic, Compass Group and Sodexo (*Annual Report* 2014/2015). Consumers are found in cafés, restaurants, hotels, travel agencies, ferries and airlines. A minor amount of coffee is distributed to customers using a private label.

Löfbergs-practitioners make a distinction between customer and consumer. Retail and out-of-home customers are purchasers of coffee; consumers are users. Treated as a guest, the consumer is supposed to experience how good it feels to have a cup of Löfbergs coffee, offered by a Löfbergs-customer (Charlotta Stenson, personal communication, October 28, 2011). As opposed to customers and consumers, competitors seem to be viewed through the lens of collective identification in a rather faceless way.

In Relation to Competitors and Customers

Intensified competition and the fact that the coffee product defines a mature market with limited growth opportunity and low profit margins have resulted in a shortened planning horizon and enhanced demand for rapid moves. Supply Chain Director Göran Sonesson (personal communication, February 6, 2015) says:

We were able to delineate a 12-month plan 15 years ago but today we have a planning horizon that looks out one month. On the Swedish retail market, Gevalia, Zoegas and Arvid Nordquist are big players and when it comes to the out-of-home market the pressure is even harder because of new actors entering the market. Demands on rapid market moves are a challenge.

On the international and global markets for coffee, Björn Forsberg, Chief Financial Officer (CFO) (personal communication, July 6, 2015), notes: 'The current trend is that coffee companies are getting bigger. Recently, Mondelëz and Master Blenders merged, forming a constellation nearly as large as Nestlé.' In addition to competitive pressure, one experiences increased pressure exerted by retail customers.

Through centralization of the purchasing functions, the retail customers have become more persuasive in their negotiations with the sales teams. Kent Pettersson is responsible for sales in the Swedish and Finnish markets. To boost Löfbergs brand recognition, sales and revenues, Pettersson and his sales team immerse themselves in numerous activities performed through sales visits, design, promotion and follow-ups of marketing campaigns. Retail sales reflect a volatile development in the global coffee market mainly due to changes in climate and supply. For the sales team the implication is that price negotiations with the customers have become an increasingly important part of sales activities (Kent Pettersson, personal communication, February 3, 2015).

Björn Forsberg (personal communication, April 7, 2012; July 6, 2015) adds:

The retail market is characterized by a few large and dominating customers. In relation to these customers we are quite small. We distribute coffee to the Swedish retail market where the largest customer has more than 50 per cent of the market. This, combined with the changing prices of raw coffee, exerts great impact on the value chain and the profitability. Raw coffee is traded on the New York Stock Exchange and the London Stock Exchange with the coffee price set in US dollar.

To give one example, at the beginning of the financial year 2011/2012, the coffee arabica price on the New York Stock Exchange was 260 cents per pound, peaking in September at 290 cents and dropping to 160 cents per pound at the end of the financial year (*Löfbergs Lila AB Annual Report* 2011/2012). Forsberg (personal communication, July 6, 2015) continues:

Fluctuations in profitability are also due to more rigid commercial restrictions. At the end of the 1990s we faced a big change in the Swedish retail market. The big customers decided to centralize their purchasing functions which enabled them to strengthening their bargaining position. Previously, we sold and distributed coffee directly to the customers. Today, customers are more knowledgeable about the market for raw coffee and exchange rate movements on the US dollar and therefore in a position to exert more influence over the final price. These changes have urged us to gauge our focus on key account management. Key account managers have been appointed, each assuming responsibility for a retail customer.

When operating in a mature market where competition is stiffening you need to have a long-term perspective and, simultaneously, be able to act in the short term. Lars Appelqvist (personal communication, August 31, 2015) clarifies this point: 'There must be a balance between short- and long-term initiatives and operations but a short-term perspective should never control the long term as long as new business opportunities can be developed in the market.' Bjorn Forsberg (personal communication, July 6, 2015) agrees:

What I experience as the brightest shining star is the long-term approach ... the business has been around for 110 years next year; the owner-family's long-term approach characterizes very much what we do. Managing for long-term profitability is important rather than for quarterly or monthly profitability. Of course there may be situations of turbulence where one must act with a short-sighted focus, unable to make investment of capital based on expectations about future returns. So, you may not always be able to maintain a long-term approach ... and you should not use the value of long-term approach as a shield to hide behind; long-term approach cannot serve as an excuse for not acting.

In response to the increased pressure exerted by competitors and customers, and regardless of geographical location, Löfbergs-practitioners immerse themselves in sustainability work, guided by the good-will values. In the exercise of moral human agency through good-willed distribution and consumption the values are kept alive. Björn Norén, Commercial Director Private Label (personal communication, February 6, 2015), submits: 'Our values cannot be reduced to a picture hung on the wall. They permeate all our activities and are kept alive in our relationships and interactions. We constantly discuss how to apply the values in our work, clarifying their practical meaning ... The good will serves as our moral compass.' Kathrine Löfberg (personal communication, June 9, 2015) points out:

We account for changes in market trends, competition, customer and consumer behaviour and the role coffee plays in different countries but our values are not subject to change. We consider how well we are known by a specific market before developing an effective way of communicating with existing and presumptive customers. Because of differences between cultures, a generic communication model cannot be applied so we discern the differences and adapt to prevailing circumstances in each country. This means that we take into account that we are completely unknown in England, quite well-known in Estonia and less so in Lithuania and Latvia. As regards sustainability ... the progress of sustainability work has been uneven in these countries ... One example regards our work in Latvia to improve energy efficiency. I would also like to mention that personnel surveys have been conducted and based on the results it is clear that our approach to work differs from the way in which the Latvians are used to do things, but, of course, local laws and rules must be followed. Not only is our "Swedish" way, the right way. Yet it is crucial to identify what matters from the point of view of our values and put the values into daily practice ... We underline the importance of living the values. Ethics and morality permeate everything we do and are not restricted to a project assigned to a department.

To communicate value-based sustainability to customers and consumers and make them appreciate certified coffee are crucial for competitive differentiation and a challenging task for Löfbergs-practitioners. 'There is tight competition for similar coffee products but our commitment and awareness of the quality of sustainability is what sets our products apart from the competitors', emphasizes Sales Director Thomas Andersson (personal communication, February 25, 2015). To encourage more customers and consumers to choose Löfbergs coffee 'requires a lot of patience', Lars Appelqvist comments (*Annual Report* 2013/2014: 3). At the time of the introduction of certified Löfbergs coffee, some scepticism prevailed towards certification as expressed among Löfbergs-practitioners, customers and consumers, acknowledged next.

In among Anders Löfberg, Middle Managers, Customers and Consumers

In the 1990s, certification gained increased attention, in particular, in association with agricultural products. The CEO at the time, owner Anders Löfberg (personal communication, November 4, 2015), saw it as necessary to make sure that coffee became certified:

The practice of organic farming emerged as an important alternative agricultural system. Reduction in the use of fertilizers and pesticides was considered necessary. I saw essential, in interaction with the middle managers, to give further impetus to this trend in connection to coffee. It was imperative to ensure that all value chain activities met certain quality criteria, from growing to consumption of coffee. The customer and the consumer must be offered certified products.

Anders Löfberg considered the discussion with the middle managers on the question of increased demands on quality and enhanced customer satisfaction through certification to be constructive. The customer and the consumer, however, did not immediately appear to be ready to buy certified coffee. Löfberg (personal communication, November 4, 2015) reveals:

At the time of the decision, the customers were not ready to buy certified coffee. But soon enough, restaurants and other out-of-home customers began to realize the need for eco-friendly products. On the consumer side, it took much longer for certified coffee to have an impact. One was more interested in the price of the product. Now, all Löfbergs coffee is certified, meaning that consumers have to buy certified coffee and even those, who, earlier on, did not show an interest in this type of coffee.

The decision taken by the CEO implied a determination to go forward with plans that did not immediately please everyone. Short-term profitability was curbed in favour of a long-term effort to offer products of the 'right' quality and, in the longer term, profitability and competitiveness. 'Yes, there were no short-term effects on earnings but long-term effects in terms of strengthened brand and enhanced competitiveness through offering the right products. These effects on profitability we greatly benefit from today', stresses Anders Löfberg (personal communication, November 4, 2015). Thomas Andersson (personal communication, February 25, 2015) emphasizes: 'Sustainability work has been carried out in a very good way and as a consequence, we have obtained a market leading position as regards sustainability. However, our competitors are trying to catch up but this far they have not ... so entrepreneurship in terms of innovative acting is what it is all about in this example.' Per Grahn, Commercial Director Out of Home (personal communication, February 25, 2015), complements the point:

And it is also about the willingness to take risks... undoubtedly we have taking risks. When we began selling certified coffee we realized that not many people knew what it was. Anders Löfberg was convinced of the need to offer certified coffee; he wondered if we could look into the eyes of the coffee farmers, honestly, and being able to sell good coffee within 30, 40 or 50 years ... So he began offering our customers certified coffee and it was expensive and the customers were not very interested but we continued offering the coffee mainly for the reason to gather information and learn. In this process, the value of entrepreneurship entwines with the value of long-term approach, constituting a starting point for certification of coffee. Investing in this process was a risky undertaking and we were in for a bumpy ride. However, when customer and consumer patterns changed and other coffee companies caught up we had already established a position. Our CEO was fully convinced that sustainability and certified coffee were the most important things one should focus on. Based on Anders Löfberg's convincement, entrepreneurship and long-term approach combine, giving our acting great credibility. I must admit, though, back then,

I really had no clue of where we were going. I did not understand why we should offer products and in some cases also lose money in the process - it was hard to understand from time to time for me.

Thomas Andersson (personal communication, February 25, 2015) agrees: 'It always takes time to increase people's awareness and getting them to start talking about sustainability ... It is a challenging task to make everybody realizing the benefits of bringing in sustainability and practising sustainability.' As entrepreneurial efforts are closely linked to risk taking (Bygrave and Minniti, 2000; Ling *et al.* 2008), there would, of course, be some hesitation in pursuing a new way of doing things, through practical evaluation extending moral human agency. According to Lars Appelqvist (personal communication, August 3, 2015):

In the short term, it is clear that a certification project requires a rather large investment but in the long run the investment would be absolutely right ... Entrepreneurial sustainable work very much builds on practitioners' long-term responsibility interlinked with commitment to give a little extra in everyday interaction ... Löfbergs-practitioners have always liked to be in the front line, involving in entrepreneurial activity by questioning current ways of doing things and practically engaging in renewed sustainability work. When we talk about entrepreneurship, it is about doing things - not different things - but doing things somewhat differently. It is about thinking creatively and in the opposite direction to our competitors.

'Initially, our customers were sceptical and dared not tell the consumers that they could offer certified coffee; instead they hid it', reveals Thomas Andersson (personal communication, February 25, 2015). Per Grahn adds:

Customers responded to our offer in a negative way. "Yes, you are welcome to sell certified coffee to us but we do not intend to tell our guests" were their words. Clearly the value of long-term approach applies. Now we are making plans for the next generation to take over the business. Long time perspectives are sometimes hard to grasp in the day-to-day perspective. I think it takes enormous strength to navigate operations, looking into a very distant future (personal communication, February 25, 2015).

From the perspective of Andersson (personal communication, February 25, 2015), 'The value of professionalism conjoins with an interest in commercial use. In other words, you should be able to generate income to thrive and survive in the long run.' Grahn (personal communication, February 25, 2015) admits:

The values of professionalism and long-term approach also entail transparency, embodying honest and open communication about our sustainability work. This has numerous commercial advantages as well. And, of course, it is necessary for us to learn about our competitors. I would also like to add, the value of long-term approach implies that the owners are free to take decisions that impose large costs over a considerable length of time.

Certified and Packed in Aluminium-Free Material Since the beginning of the 1990s, the share of vacuum packaging has increased and glass jars have been replaced by PET cans and zip bags. Certified coffee is distributed in packages using aluminium-free material. Charlotta Stenson (*Get to Know a Good Coffee* 2013: 11) points out, 'As one of the industry's packaging pioneers, we are constantly working to come up with even smarter and more environmentally friendly packaging.' A more recently tested alternative is plastic made of sugar canes. The intention is to replace the fossil-based plastic. Sustainability Director Eva Eriksson highlights (personal communication, February 13, 2015):

We were the first in Sweden, in 1993, to remove the laminate with aluminium in the packaging, which required investing in a new packaging line to run the new material – a completely aluminium-free laminate. The material was as much as 20 per cent more expensive. It was one of the biggest decisions Anders Löfberg made at the time. The governor of the province of Värmland was here and physically pressed the button to turn on the power of the very first new-line machine. That was a great moment!

Engaging entrepreneurship, Löfbergs-practitioners develop and test new techniques and material to be able to provide more energy-efficient and sustainable solutions in the future. Since 2005, the climate impact regarding emission of greenhouse gases has been reduced by 24 per cent through the use of renewable energy. The goal is a reduction of 40 per cent by 2020 and a decrease of dependence on fossil fuels. The goal is 100 per cent renewable energy by 2020 (*Annual Report* 2014/2015). Apparently it is all about being 'enviropreneurial'. Generally employed in the literature on marketing, the term 'enviropreneurial' means formulating and implementing entrepreneurial and environmentally beneficial policies, procedures and practices (Dean and McMullen 2007; Menon and Menon 1997). As a consequence of people's perseverance in sustainability work, all Löfbergs coffee products are certified today and this work can be ascribed an enviropreneurial character.

As all coffee under the Löfbergs brand now is certified and packed in aluminium-free material, one hopes, of course, that an increasing number of customers and consumers will realize that certified coffee is worth for the price. Large out-of-home customers such as Sodexo, Nordic Choice and Compass Group, through their choice of Löfbergs coffee, have already chosen sustainability.

'When Sodexo chose Löfbergs, they increased from 2 to 53 per cent Fairtrade in a year. This resulted in slightly more than SEK 1.5 million for coffee farmers and cooperatives' (*Annual Report* 2013/2014: 30). 'As part of the corporate responsibility roadmap, the so-called Better Tomorrow Plan, Sodexo buys sustainable and organic labelled coffee. Löfbergs is Sodexo's main supplier of coffee in Scandinavia', reports Eva Kristensson, Head of Brand & Communications Nordics, Sodexo (personal communication, June 9, 2016).

In 2015, Löfbergs earned the Nordic Choice Hotels Sustainability Award. Nordic Choice Hotels is one of the largest hotel chains in Scandinavia. The award committee stated: 'Löfbergs has worked for a long time with sustainability and always puts ethic, social responsibility and environment first. There are few that work with sustainability as whole-heartedly and consistent as Löfbergs. The company strengthens us in our sustainability work and enables us to free up resources to focus on areas where the needs are greater' (*Annual Report* 2014/2015: 15). Cathrine Dehli, Director of Sustainability at Nordic Choice Hotels, Oslo, Norway (personal communication, July 5, 2016), clarifies:

The Gro Harlem Brundtland definition of sustainable development provides the basis for our definition of sustainability. For us, this means that we must operate in a way that, simultaneously, takes care of people, the environment and the profitability of our business. We should, in other words, conduct our business in a way that allows next generations to meet their needs. Ethics and morality are an integral part of our business. We do not believe that we are able to generate and maintain profitability without caring for people and environment, and we believe also that we have a responsibility and an obligation to work with this. We cannot be indifferent as to how we run our business. The Suppler Code of Conduct exemplifies our concerns for ethics and morality.

The sustainability award is an award that Nordic Choice Hotels gives one of its suppliers who has distinguished itself when it comes to environmental, climate or social conditions, and who is able to do this in a way that also protects profitability. Löfberg is our only contract provider on coffee, but one of the very best suppliers on sustainability as we see it. Löfbergs chooses solutions that are sustainable and that will ensure profitability in the future.

A recent addition to the list of customers serving organic and Fairtrade-certified coffee are Helsinki Theatre and HK Areena in Turku, Finland (*Annual Report* 2013/2014).

Teamwork, Coordination and Integration

Teamwork, coordination and integration of value chain activities communicate sustainability goals and are ways to make sure that distribution and consumption allow for customer and consumer satisfaction.

However, as Eva Eriksson (personal communication, February 13, 2015) reveals:

Previously we were not particularly good at communicating sustainability goals. So our CEO put his foot down through the decision to conduct a thorough investigation of our present sustainability work. Effective cross-functional teamwork resulted in a to-do-list, specifying actions to take in areas such as purchasing, processing, marketing, logistics, communication and Human Resources. Our enhanced focus on sustainability developmental work entails tough goals and in 2012, a new position was established: Sustainability Director. This position was assumed by me. As Sustainability Director I coordinate sustainability work across functions, departments, business areas and subsidiaries. This includes responsibility for environmental performance, making sure that the requirements for the ISO 14001 environmental management system are fulfilled in business operations and further, responsibility for reduction of energy use, improvement in packaging material, formulation and implementation of a business ethics policy and other policies and a whistleblower system. By participating in a workshop, led by Paul Sharma from the Academy of Human Rights in Business, CSR Sweden, I learned how to design a policy for ethical business conduct. Ensuing discussions with colleagues at departments, sales conferences and kick-off events resulted in the presentation of a policy document, signed by all Löfbergs employees.

Under the management of Eva Eriksson, Åsa Lindqvist, Mechanical Engineer and Production Technician, coordinates activities regarding hygiene, safety, environment and security, activities that also include internal audit. She works with the quality management system including ISO 14001, the standard for providing tools to manage environmental responsibilities; ISO 9001, a quality standard; and ISO 22000, a standard with a focus on food safety management and control. Written procedures in the management system, for example, the procedure for waste collection and disposal, evacuation and emergency escape must comply with the requirements set by the different standards, legal and other requirements. Lindqvist (personal communication, October 12, 2012) relates:

As a member of a team that focuses on sustainability, I am involved in discussions on how to measure sustainability and ensure that the whole chain of activities, growing, processing and distribution of coffee, is made sustainable. Life cycle analyses have been conducted. Most challenging is that sustainability activities contain many aspects difficult to measure. Since the beginning of the 1990s, numerous actions have been taken but there are still areas where we can do better ... we are currently in the process of defining indicators that are relevant for measuring sustainability and provide good feedback.

The integrated approach to sustainability work is a prerequisite for good-willed distribution and consumption, which entail communicating to the customer and the consumer the values of responsibility, commitment, a long-term approach, entrepreneurship and professionalism. In a mature market, characterized by low profit margins and limited expansion possibilities, customer and consumer habits are rather firmly rooted. The integrated approach to sustainability work thus too implies training sessions through which the customer and the consumer are encouraged to learn about the raw material, how to brew coffee, ways to work smart and reduce waste and the advantages of buying certified Löfbergs coffee. Specialty Coffee Manager Anna Nordström (personal communication, August 4, 2015) runs these sessions, at which she stresses the need to understand the great impact raw material has on the aroma and taste of coffee: 'I am passionate about making customers and consumers discover the wonderful world of coffee, realizing that there are numerous nuances of aroma and taste, and understanding how crucial the raw material is for aroma and taste.' The aroma and taste of coffee, much like those of wine, depend on its source. 'Coffee and wine are more alike than coffee and tea. As with grapes, every nuance possible can be affected by the earth and climate from which coffee comes' (Sinnott 2010: 7). Nordström (personal communication, August 4, 2015) adds, 'And the more you learn about coffee, the more interesting coffee becomes. So I am passionate about encouraging people to test new flavours and play a little with grades of grinding and brewing.'

Recently authorized as Sensory Professional by Specialty Coffee Association of Europe (SCAE), Anna Nordström is the first trainer in Sweden in coffee sensory, skilled in sensory evaluation of coffee, which implies expertise in distinguishing between a variety of coffee qualities and flavours, for example. She comments (Press Release, August 31, 2016: 1):

It is certainly a feather in my cap and something that carries a lot of weight within the world of specialty coffee but the most important is that we at Löfbergs now have an even deeper knowledge about flavours. It will strengthen us internally and make it possible for us to further develop our training offer. To be the only coffee business in Sweden that offers training in sensory skills is of course valuable and important.

In the words of Björn Norén, Commercial Director Private Label, (personal communication, February 6, 2015):

The values are expressed through the sustainability work performed in integration with all activities of the value chain, from bean to cup. And even if a product is bought from another producer, a careful check is carried out to see whether the producer's value chain, from raw material to end product, meets our sustainability-based criteria. So our values also apply to another producer.

Kathrine Löfberg (personal communication, June 9, 2015) interjects:

Discussions at department meetings concern how to integrate the values into our activities. The sales teams explain the meaning of acting professionally in encounters with the customers. Everyone must explain what the values mean to them and concretize the values in their actions and interactions and be aware that the values can be used in situations where tensions and conflicts emerge. When confronting misconduct in the behaviour of a co-worker, the supervisor should ask: Do you think your acting is consistent with our vales – to what extent is the acting professional? You must live the values always.

Teamwork, coordination and integration are also enabled by a current project concerning the launching of two new products in parallel. It involves a team of practitioners, representing different functions, departments, business areas and subsidiaries of the Löfbergs Group. Norén (personal communication, February 6, 201) reveals:

The work is based on a project plan and a checklist of activities that make explicit the values and practically proceeds in accordance with the so-called lock model. Akin to seaway locks with beams routinely raised above the sea level for enabling ships to pass through, we use lock as a symbolic devise to raise or lower our work, designating critical decision points. When a phase of our project work is approved by the top management team we get through a lock, if not, we must reconsider and adjust our work. The steering committee of the project, including members of the top management team, together with the project leaders discuss activities to be performed and corrections to be made. The lock model offers means for control and quality assurance. Within six months after finalizing the project, customer reactions are investigated and evaluated. The project work is entrepreneurial in a sense ... it builds on extensive coordination across boundaries between functions, departments, business areas and subsidiaries of the Löfbergs Group. It is an exciting and challenging task for me as the project owner, on the basis of our values, to provide for integration, advancing our efforts in the same direction to reach our targets.

A Good Reason to Meet

Consumption suggests meetings between consumers, 'experiencing not only the aroma and taste of Löfbergs coffee but also how good it feels in the heart to drink Löfbergs coffee' (Charlotta Stenson, personal communication, October 28, 2011). 'Coffee is important with regard to the social aspect; it brings pleasure and joy' (Kathrine Löfberg personal communication, November 28, 2011). 'And when thinking about coffee my mouth is watering ... you hardly ever ask for a cup of coffee without a smile on your face ... coffee will make you happy in a way ... "coffee-happy" I would say, and for me, coffee is Löfbergs coffee' (Eva Eriksson personal communication, February 13, 2015). All these comments presume that Löfbergs coffee is a good reason to meet. Kathrine Löfberg (personal communication, June 9, 2015) clarifies, 'The word "good" has two meanings; it signifies a pleasant and enjoyable meeting and represents high-quality criteria of sustainability.'

Two cafés, Rosteriet in Karlstad and Café Löfbergs in Stockholm, have been established. Anders Löfberg (personal communication, November 4, 2015) acknowledges:

Based on the broadened view of coffee, the business concept now encompasses cafés, located in Karlstad and Stockholm. Today coffee is drunk in many different places and at different times of the day which has required an expansion of our assortment. You may feel good about medium roasted coffee in the morning and dark roasted in the evening; a variety of coffees are offered all day, especially due to the existence of caffeine caps and capsule machines.

The café Rosteriet in Karlstad opened on September 1, 2011. Consumption of Löfbergs coffee in this café entails special roasting and provides the guest with the opportunity to learn about where and how coffee beans are grown. At a visit to the café I was informed that coffee from Honduras is prepared in a special way through blending pressed coffee with filtered coffee, that it has grown on the slopes of a mountain and that the name of the owner of the plantation is Hector. Moreover, I was informed about the character of the coffee. Because the beans are cultivated at a plantation in the highland areas and dried for a long time, fruit characteristics emerge. Charlotta Stenson (personal communication, October 28, 2011) complements:

The guest should feel welcomed ... a great deal of our work aims at increasing the respect for coffee – coffee is not just a drink. It can tell us a lot. There are many different tastes and origins and coffee is very much like wine ... In the world of wines, passionate stories build on a rich language of origins and flavours but that kind of language is not yet used in connection with coffee. If a coffee plant has grown on fertile volcanic soil it brings out a specific tone ...We welcome the guest, that is, the consumer with this kind of stories; we wish also to awaken the consumer's curiosity to test various types of coffee.

Rosteriet is not merely an ordinary café but a café that offers extensive service, requiring the employees to interact with the guests and provide an informative background, both orally and through a description on a storyboard, to the coffee being served. The café worker tells about the country where the coffee is produced and the specific plantation where it was grown and describes taste and character.

Also in other cafés in Karlstad, Löfbergs coffee gives you a good reason to meet. Coop is one of the largest retail customers of Löfbergs. Coop runs grocery retail trade in chains like Stora Coop and Coop Extra. Stora

Coop in Karlstad is dedicated to offering the customers a range of products from local suppliers. It is of great advantage to the Coop Café (at Stora Coop) to have access to a local roaster such as Löfbergs. 'We know that our customers prefer products of known origin from the local area. To match our customers' needs we offer Löfbergs coffee', says Chef Pontus Boman (personal communication, August 30, 2016).

During the summer, Löfbergs coffee is served at the café called Sluss-vakten ('The Lockmaster'). During the nineteenth century, a man with the title 'lockmaster' lived in the house where the café is located, near the canal with locks regulating the height of the water for enabling the passage of boats. Pointed out by Director Elisabeth Ringdahl Wik (personal communication, June 6, 2016):

It is important that the coffee tastes good and is ethically sourced. It should be ecologically grown and Fairtrade-certified. We have decided to offer brewed coffee only, it fits the environment very well. The café is situated in the old house in which the Lockmaster once lived, in the 1870s. It is a kind of environment that creates an ambience that especially your Grandma would enjoy.

King Creole is not just any café, according to the owner Gun Nyström (personal communication, June 9, 2016):

Here it is mostly about Elvis. In addition to coffee you can buy Elvis souvenirs and listen to Elvis music. We serve Löfbergs coffee mainly for the reason of the local thing ... Löfbergs is located geographically close to us. In addition, the coffee tastes good. Of course it is also important to choose Fairtrade and organic coffee.

The library building in Karlstad houses Café Selma. On the wall, to the right of the counter, there is a sign that catches the eye of the café guest. Equipped with the Löfbergs logotype, coloured in purple, it conveys a specific message: 'Eradicate poverty over a cup of coffee!' An additional sign reads, 'Here we serve really good coffee.' Café worker Filippa Löfgren Orebjörk (personal communication, June 9, 2016) explains:

We offer our guests organic and good coffee. The sign hung on the wall provides the guest with information related to Löfbergs coffee. Coffee is served in cups made of porcelain and in disposable cups made out of paper and all are marked with the Löfbergs logotype. The paper napkins, matching the cups, are printed with text in purple that reads: "A good reason to meet".'

Tord Karlsson (personal communication, June 9, 2016), a regular guest at the Café Selma, reveals: 'I am not specifically concerned about the label of the coffee I consume ... and whether it is marked Löfbergs or not. My only concern is that the coffee I buy is Fairtrade and organic.'

In the café named Swenströmskas Stone Oven Bakery, a sign is hung on the wall behind the counter, telling the guest that certified Löfbergs coffee is served. Owner Moa Näsström (personal communication, September 13, 2016) points out:

Our ecological profile is really important to us; in addition, the geographical proximity to Löfbergs. It provides us with a quick and easy way to meet with and get support from our supplier of coffee. It is great to have Löfbergs in town! And we should all be proud of having such an excellent and environmentally responsible coffee roaster in Karlstad. We are communicating to our café guests orally, and also in written form through the text on the wall and on the coffee thermoses, that we serve Löfbergs coffee.

Unfolding Moral Human Agency – Commentary (II)

As indicated in this section, good-willed practising, constituted of distribution and consumption activities, unfolds moral human agency in the projective and practical-evaluative dimensions. There is strong focus on sustainability work, which under the guidance of the good-will values (responsibility, commitment, long-term approach, entrepreneurship and professionalism) is carried out through teamwork among Löfbergs-practitioners, coordination, integration, controls and follow-ups of distribution and consumption activities. What lies before the Löfbergs-practitioners in terms of satisfied customers and consumers, buying certified coffee packed in aluminium-free material, actualizes the projective and the practical-evaluative dimensions and includes the competitor.

Present future-oriented activities introduce a view of a sustainable future that sets the Löfbergs coffee apart from the coffee offered by the competitors. The competitors can only be viewed through a depersonalized lens based on a collective identification (cf. Brewer and Gardner 1996). Their in-betweens make competitive differentiation through a focus on value-based sustainability a necessity. Faced with intensified competition, the practitioners projectively construct an image of where to go while making practical normative judgements. The sustainability work proffers a reconsideration of past ways of doing things, engaging the practical-evaluative dimension. Normative claims are pronounced through using the good-will values as a moral compass. The values are seen as conducive to sustainability work and generation of competitive advantage.

In relation to the increased pressure from competitors operating in national, international and global markets, the practitioners experience a planning horizon severely shortened. Here 'market' appears as a given structure. From a temporal-relational horizon, market is rather a context that emerges as Löfbergs-practitioners relate to the competitors by exercising moral agency through immersing themselves in sustainability work. Although rooted in past behaviour (Johnson, Smith and Codling 2010), agency suggests a tacit social accommodation of structure (Cambell-Hunt 2007) that has implications for how we view market. Agency refers to human potentiality (Whittington 2015), and new practices can emerge over time through practitioners' improvisation (Orlikowski 1996). To both Giddens (1979) and Bourdieu (1990) practices are continuously defined and redefined between the objectified and the objectifying intention. In other words, the performative aspect of agency creates, maintains and modifies the ostensive aspect, as Feldman and Pentland (2003) point out (Chapter 2).

Yet, we need to go further, emphasizing the temporal and relational in connection with practical-evaluative agency. Agency is then not overshadowed by pre-established ends and shaped by the duality of agency and structure that implicates a mutual constitutive relationship between the performative and the ostensive, and the micro and the macro. The practical-evaluative dimension locates agency in the contextualization of social experience. Moral human agency in the practical-evaluative dimension is performed through problematization and critical deliberation with others 'about the pragmatic and normative exigencies of lived situations' (Emirbayer and Mische 1998: 994). This suggests that for highlighting temporal-relational dynamics of agency in relation to 'market' we could use 'marketization', which, according to Çalişkan and Callon (2010), accounts for how the market dynamically forms. Since information on in-betweens among Löfbergs-practitioners and representatives of competitors is lacking to a great extent it is impossible, however, to take a closer look at marketization.

Face-to-face interactions take place among Löfbergs-practitioners and customers, and between customers and consumers. As pointed out, practitioners have become increasingly immersed in negotiations with the retail customers. The move from decentralized to centralized purchasing has implications for their reciprocal relationship, calling on the practical-evaluative dimension. The practitioners are required to reinterpret past habitual ways of interacting with the customers. What occurs at present tends to involve levelling-out knowledge differences between them, reducing disparities. The retail customers apparently increase their capacity for action.

Activities related to coffee certification train the spotlight on Anders Löfberg, not as a separate individual, but as a self extending in relations to and in interactions with middle managers, customers and coffee farmers. Primarily engaging the practical-evaluative dimension, Löfberg in interaction with the middle managers shaped present responses to an emerging sustainable future, announcing normative claims on eco-friendly distribution and consumption of coffee. Because certification did not improve profits immediately and contribute customer satisfaction, some middle managers and customers expressed scepticism as to the decision to certify the coffee. The practical-evaluative dimension thus also makes us aware of the difficulty of achieving reciprocity in the giving and receiving for the short term, leaving the asymmetry temporarily unresolved among Anders Löfberg, some middle managers and customers. Today, not very sceptical about certified Löfbergs coffee, the customer provides the consumer a good reason to meet by serving Löfbergs coffee, exhibited by the examples of consumption in cafés in Karlstad. The café customer residing in the city of Karlstad also places a high value on spatial accessibility to the roaster of Löfbergs coffee.

It is also acknowledged that material plays a role in good-willed distribution and consumption. Arguably, the value of entrepreneurship, integral to moral human agency, is effectuated through the development and use of aluminium-free material, the replacement of glass jars by PET cans and zip bags and the testing of other material with the intention to replace fossil-based plastic. As marked by Commentary (I) in connection to growing, transportation and processing, material helps to extend human agency in the projective and practical-evaluative dimensions.

In Continuous Interaction with a Value-Laden Past

Löfbergs-practitioners continuously interact with a value-laden past, reinterpreted and effectuated at present. This past is associated with the story of the three founding brothers, Anders, John and Joseph Löfberg, representing the first generation of the Löfberg family. Retold, the story walks us down memory lane, illustrating far-off occurrences. It contains a reference to a company with the name 'Bröderna Löfberg AB' and pulls a package of coffee in the purple colour into our view. The purple colour calls on the past and pronounces also a future 'intention' while delineating 'the Purple road to success' and directing attention to 'the Purple question' in terms of vision, strategy and goals.

In recognition of present practising that nonlinearly communicates with a past through which a future is drawn up for instilling a sense of intention in everyone, the iterational dimension of moral human agency is made explicit. The iterational dimension adds to our understanding of moral human agency that so far has been limited to a projective and practical-evaluative temporal relationality.

From One Generation to the Next

The three brothers Anders, John and Joseph started up a business, registered in 1906 under the name of 'Bröderna Löfberg AB'. So the company has been operating for a long time, celebrating the 110th anniversary in 2016. Anders Löfberg (personal communication, January 9, 2012) tells:

Expansion and growth led to changes in the business concept. Starting out as a local company it offered a wide range of groceries to retailers operating in the two neighbouring provinces of Värmland and Dalsland. From 1911, the coffee business began to pick up on the increased demand for roasted coffee and the business concept centred its focus on roasted coffee. Earlier on it fell on the customer to do the roasting. Each household and store was equipped with a roasting machine. In the 1920s, we packed coffee, using different labels for delivery of different types of coffee. What we today call brands, back then were different mixtures of coffee, separated in colour-coded bags ... one product was purple-coloured and called "Löfbergs Luxury Blend" and was assigned the number of 35 ... it turned out to be the most popular product, outcompeting all other products included in the offering of groceries. This meant that marketing now focused on the purple product. The coffee market grew and in 1927, the three founding brothers decided to split the business into three separate units, coffee, wholesale and import of Citroën cars. It felt natural to do so since each brother was already managing a specific part. The coffee business, managed by my grandfather Anders, expanded. Eventually the wholesale unit was acquired by the local wholesaler M. Österberg, later acquired by "Handelskompaniet", a trading company based in the city of Jönköping, situated in the southern part of Sweden in the province of Småland. In the 1970s, the regional wholesalers were united and included in Dagab.

The first generation is my grandfather Anders. I do not know how much time he actually spent on coffee business operations but he obviously handled the business very well. He was also the President of the Mission Church in Karlstad and as a liberal he engaged in local politics. The second generation is my father Åke. When my grandfather passed away, the company was owned by Åke in co-ownership with his mother and brother. In 1949 or 1950, the co-owners were bought out and Åke became the sole owner. Clearly, this was a key turning point in the business ... Åke was the lonely entrepreneur, who now could make his own decisions without asking for others' consent which enabled boldness and originality in decision making. This was probably needed for finding ways to respond quickly to the restructuring that then took place in the coffee industry and face the intensified competition. During World War II, the Swedish coffee roasters jointly imported coffee beans. At that point in time, there were around 140 roasters but many of those were unable to restart after the war ended and were closed down.

One example of Åke's boldness is the construction, in 1949, of a new building, a big step for a small local company used to roast coffee in old warehouse buildings. Åke was courageous enough to acquire new machines and equipment to improve efficiency and provide more rational production solutions. It was important to arrange production in long series while maintaining the right level of quality. Changes in production brought to bear on marketing, adding strength and competitive advantage. For sure, the purple colour held it all together, the entire business. Everything went very well for Åke. Around 1956, he made plans for a considerably larger roaster. In interaction with me, my brother and sister, he explained clearly that he paid our grandmother and uncle very well when taking over the business and becoming its sole owner. At that moment in life, he was penniless but thanks to good relationship with the local bank he received some financial support. Undoubtedly, he was confronted with a high-risk situation, regarding, on the one hand, the ownership change, and on the other, the expansion of production through investments in new machinery, methods and larger facilities.

Referring to past changes in the market for coffee, Löfberg (personal communication, January 9, 2012) discloses:

Since the 1920s, the market for coffee expanded with an exception for a decrease during World War II. I think it was in 1942, imports of coffee beans declined considerably and we received only 18 per cent of original imports to Sweden. Market rationing was mainly due to foreign currency restrictions. A few years after the war, free trade of coffee was implemented which facilitated market growth for Löfbergs coffee. Gradually the business grew. My father Åke, CEO from 1945, established branches with sale offices, many of which were relatively small businesses, called 'nederlag" ("defeats"). There were seven or eight defeats operating independently. Spread from northern to southern Sweden, located in the cities of Skellefteå, Gävle, Sundsvall, Växjö, Jönköping and Malmö, for example. In order to coordinate and better align marketing activities, a decision was made to take over the defeats. And it was at that point in time, in the 1960s, I began to show an interest in the coffee business. Already in the 1950s, offices of our own were set up in Gothenburg and Stockholm for distribution of coffee. Up until the millennium shift and the year 2000, we used a direct chain of distribution to serve our store customers; retail customers were handled by wholesalers. For the past ten to twelve years, growth has been accomplished through acquisitions. Increasingly, the customers are Nordic and a way to meet their needs and requirements, withstanding competition, is to collaborate across national borders.

Already as a teenager, Anders Löfberg participated in business meetings that dealt with strategic issues. While still at school he gained rich experience from working in different departments. Brother Jan worked with sales. The sister and brother-in-law became involved as owners. However, sustaining ownership of the Löfbergs business was not of particular interest to them. In the 1990s, they were bought out by Anders and Jan, who now each owned one-third of the business, the remaining part shared among their children.

Anders Löfberg; his wife, Monika; brother and sister represent the third generation. 'My wife was not formally employed but involved in everything.

She travelled around the world with me, raised five children while, at the same time, representing the business', Löfberg reveals (personal communication, November 4, 2015). The fourth generation consists of six people: the five children of Anders and Monica Löfberg, Kathrine, Helen, Martin, Therese and Niklas, and the son of Jan Löfberg, Mikael. They are all members of the Board of Directors, showing great interest in ownership, taking long-term responsibility for ensuring generational renewal. Kathrine, Therese and Niklas also directly involve themselves in business activities. Löfberg (personal communication, January 9, 2012) adds:

It felt quite natural for the children to be associated with the business. Kathrine told me, if earlier on, she had realized the enjoyment of working here, she would have started earlier. We have a rule that says you should not be going straight from school to our company but gain independence and self-integrity through work in another industry for five years. This means that you will be able to bring some new blood into the family business.

Ever since 1999, Kathrine Löfberg has been involved in a variety of strategizing activities associated with, for example, export, establishment of a subsidiary, acquisitions, communication, marketing, and brand positioning in markets in Sweden and abroad. On January 1, 2015, she succeeded her father as Chairman of the Board of Directors (Kathrine Löfberg, personal communication, November 28, 2011; June 9, 2015). The year before, the Löfbergs Board lost a key member. Jan Löfberg, who had been actively involved in the business throughout his life, died in 2014 (Anders Löfberg, personal communication, November 4, 2015).

Ranked by age, the Löfberg family defines a hierarchy of members, but a more accurate description of the family accounts for betweenness in terms of joint ownership, collaboration and closeness, infused with the values of responsibility, commitment, a long-term approach, entrepreneurship and professionalism. Kathrine Löfberg (personal communication, June 9, 2015) comments:

Yes, I am the big sister ... a family can represent some form of hierarchy ... All family members have worked tightly together with a focus on ownership issues and we have come up with a forecast called "Next 2050". It originates in our values and questions about the advantages of joint ownership of the business, overall goals and how far ahead we can look. For several years, these questions have been dwelled on, driven us more closely together. Our generation, which consists of my sisters and brothers and a cousin, has been provided equal opportunity to engage in the operations of the business. Regardless of being the big sister or the little sister, the presumption of equality allows everyone's voice to be heard and respected. So a hierarchy cannot be applied to our family ... we may hold different views on an issue, yet in my capacity as the big sister I am not able to exert more influence over the issue in question than anyone else.

By working tightly together, being anchored in the history of previous generations, one develops an understanding of how to do business. Although it can be argued in accordance with CEO Lars Appelqvist (personal communication, August 31, 2015) that 'Anders has "passed on" the values to his children', the activity of 'passing on' entails social-ization very much in terms of tacit understanding and involvement in everyday activity. A 'transmission' of values is rather a question of unin-tended progression, yet with an element of 'detectable purposiveness' discernible in the stream of business activities (Haag 2012: 65). Haag (2012) points to socialization as central for understanding succession in family business, not as an option but as on ongoing process through which family members learn. This means that succession is not necessarily planned and designed but evolves over time as family members exchange experiences and continuously learn about how to do business while also drawing on 'external' sources for inspiration and renewal. Anders Löfberg (personal communication, November 4, 2015) emphasizes:

Today, Swedish industry is faced with the giant problem of continuity – a family business needs to promote continual renewal across generations. Far too often a family business lacks a family member willing to engage in the business … this might be due to the fact that family members have not been sufficiently involved in the business and have missed building commitment over time. Besides, they might only hear about what is troublesome and cumbersome and not about the enjoyable and fun parts … I have tried to inspire my children and grandchildren and it is not that difficult considering the specific product we offer. Almost everyone drinks coffee … However, it has not been completely natural that they all should involve in the business. While working here during summer vacations, they have been given the opportunity to learn about the business. But I have been extremely concerned that they should not spend too much time working here when growing up. They should be aware of the wider environment of the business and the world we live in, encouraged to come up with new ideas, bringing fresh blood into the business.

The value of professionalism is made explicit through the words of Löfberg (personal communication, November 4, 2015) about the importance of keeping some distance between himself and the children and grandchildren:

Yes, most importantly, in consideration of the individual's independent growth … you are supposed to be able to face challenges and deal with different problems that arise in a workplace without the father providing shelter, without being protected by the sphere of the father, hiding under his wings. When employed, you are expected to comply with the same rules as everyone else. The terms and conditions of employment and the performance curve equally apply to all employees regardless of kinship ties and ownership in the business.

Karlstad is a place attributed a significant role in the process of socialization, adding a geographical aspect to socialization. It also includes the symbol that 'the sun of your life is the coffee in Karlstad'. The former CEO and Chairman of the Board of Directors (personal communication, November 4, 2015) points to this symbol and the geographical location of Karlstad:

There is no academic education that helps generate your knowledge on coffee and roasting. Training is offered here in Karlstad. At one specific place you learn about coffee and how to process coffee. This creates stability and there is no need for roaming about the country. You just stay here and grow with the business – this is essential, I think.

Even if you remain in the sunlight of Karlstad, your horizon is not limited in space and time. Lars Appelqvist (personal communication, August 31, 2015) refers to the Löfbergs legacy, imperative to honour, maintain and keep alive in the future, which requires effectuating the value of a long-term approach:

Anders always temporally frames a question, acknowledging the advantages of having a time horizon that extends well over decades ... He is quite unique in his way of being ... he thinks in decades and very few would have the ability to do that. Sometimes it is difficult to translate this thinking to present practicing; you wonder why you should apply such a perspective ... Even if I consider myself pretty good at looking far ahead there is no comparison to Anders.

The Löfbergs legacy instils a sense of intention, not only in practitioners who share biological ancestors, but in everyone since 'we all consider ourselves to be somewhat of coffee specialists and ambassadors for Löfbergs coffee', submits the present CEO (personal communication, August 31, 2015).

Instilling a Sense of Intention

Referring to the Löfbergs legacy, Lars Appelqvist (personal communication, August 31, 2015) highlights:

The Löfbergs legacy instils in us a strong sense of intention ... we have been talking a lot about intention. The coffee sector focuses much on coffee roasting but roasting is nothing unique. You can roast coffee in a certain way, yet a more exciting question is why you do it. The intention of being involved in coffee roasting is intimately entwined with the owners' vision for 2050. So it is not only about achieving a stable financial position in the future but also about the broader issue of "intention" and a delineation of a future track of practicing that involves everyone.

'Our ambition is to promote a positive work environment where everyone feels encouraged to actively participate, ensuring that no one is excluded or trampled on', Kathrine Löfberg (personal communication, June 9, 2015) emphasizes. Collaborative closeness, in association with 'sympathy', seems to be a key.

It can be contended that 'intention' opens up to numerous in-betweens among Löfbergs-practitioners, allowing for sympathy in terms of a fellow-feeling, to use Hutcheson's (2007) expression. By means of fellow-feeling, practitioners construct a pleasurable ambience while effectuating the good-will values. In a good-will sense, sympathy is styled as benevolence, brotherly love, compassion and gratitude, for example (Bentham 1988). Iterationally, fellow-feeling calls on a past that 'speaks' of the Löfberg family and especially Anders Löfberg. Embodying the good-will values, he was always available to his co-workers, enabling closeness and sharing of experience and ideas through direct dialogue. Löfberg (personal communication, November 4, 2015) comments: 'Well, Swedish leadership is participatory in character; it is based on mutual respect and collaboration between leaders and their staff. An employee who performs well and achieves good results needs to be recognized and confirmed by a leader through praise and feedback.'

Löfbergs-practitioners not related to the Löfberg family by blood or included through marriage bear witness to the collaborative closeness in relation to the Löfberg family. Specialty Coffee Manager Anna Nordström (personal communication, August 4, 2015) reveals: 'Every day I meet with members of the owner family ... tasting coffee, for instance. Physical presence of the owners permits closeness. When you have the opportunity for face-to-face interaction, looking directly into their eyes, a close relationship is established characterized by trust and mutual respect.' From the experience of Supply Chain Director Göran Sonesson (personal communication, February 6, 2015), 'Continuous face-to-face communication – with strong confidence built into the relationship with Anders Löfberg – has contributed to a sense of belongingness to a Löfbergs world of practising.' In the words of Commercial Director Out of Home Per Grahn (personal communication, February 25, 2015): 'Many things have changed over the past decades ... however, changes have not occurred to our values, they prevail. The business is still family-owned with the family's values deeply ingrained and serving as guiding principles of our activities. For me, this is the chief reason for staying in my job after 18 years of employment.' CFO Björn Forsberg (personal communication, July 6, 2015) too testifies about the availability of the former CEO and Chairman in an account that reflects great admiration for him:

I think there is an advantage in having the opportunity to make a quick decision when needed, which is due to the closeness to the owner-family. When handling a financial matter that requires a visit to the bank I can easily ask a member of the family to accompany me … this is also an example of strong confidence built in our relationship … it is part of the charm with this type of business, absolutely, and definitely part of the meaning of working here. Besides … preparation for the fourth generation to take over is under way. At our gathering in August, 2014, Anders Löfberg announced that he was handing over the chairmanship for the coffee business to his eldest daughter – he will continue to be involved in the real estate business. At this specific gathering, Anders received a standing ovation which tells a lot … I think many of us experience that we somehow work for Anders personally … people show immense loyalty to him. His long engagement with the business means that he has exerted much influence over the business and its development and it is all because he is the person he is, enjoying everyone's admiration and respect. There is a unique connection to Anders, especially felt by people having worked here much longer than I have, for 30 or 40 years … extreme loyalty has been developed to Anders.

Anders Löfberg (personal communication, November 4, 2015) summarizes: 'I have been a CEO for 25 years … by exercising the open door policy I always made myself accessible to my co-workers. Also, I often walked around in the factory, talking with and listening to people while checking out that everything ran smoothly.'

'It is a fantastic business, considering the fact that the values prevail', highlights Sales Director Thomas Andersson (personal communication, February 25, 2015). Lars Appelqvist (personal communication, August 31, 2015) adds:

Yes, the values are built into the walls and Anders Löfberg embodies very much the values, setting the tone for our way of being. Not figuring in the foreground, he always acts in the background, allowing each one of us to make our voice heard, giving credit where credit is due. The owners live in strong integrity and represent a professionalism that acknowledges your efforts and achievements rather than the amount of years you have been employed. This contributes mutual respect. You communicate openly what is good and what is bad. The value web creates the foundation for this. And I must admit that I had no idea how things were done when I first arrived here. The values help to eliminate doings that do not align with them and people who fail to live the values leave. Apparently, we seem to attract a certain type of people.

Both Thomas Andersson (personal communication, February 25, 2015) and Per Grahn (personal communication, February 25, 2015) apply the terms 'genuine' and 'fair' in describing how it is to live a Löfbergs life. Supply Chain Director Göran Sonesson (personal communication, February 6, 2015) too notes:

The Löfbergs life is very much about values and Anders Löfberg personifies the values. My upbringing laid a moral foundation; my parents taught me the difference between right and wrong. My own values align in harmony with the values articulated and lived by the Löfberg family, representing a morality of treating other people as you wish to be treated yourself without putting anyone at disadvantage ... And the focus on coffee just gives me a very good feeling. More specifically it is about how you act, treating others honestly and with respect. There is considerable openness in what we do; we are inspired to take initiatives and try out new ways of practising and there is closeness in our relationships. It is easy to bring up various matters for discussion and decision making channels are very short.

From the perspective of Björn Forsberg (personal communication, July 6, 2015), 'The owners' unprecedented proximity and availability are something extremely positive.'

Back in the 1920s, a package coloured in purple contained the first best-selling coffee, Löfbergs Luxury Blend. Since then, 'purple' has been strongly associated with the Löfbergs business and brand, and is the first colour granted a patent in connection to coffee. It should also be noted, according to Per Grahn (personal communication, February 25, 2015), that a perfectly matured coffee cherry is purple. From a historical perspective, as earlier posited by Anders Löfberg (personal communication, January 9, 2012), 'the purple colour held it all together, the entire business.' Johan Eriksson, Process Operator and Club Chairman of the Swedish Food Workers' Union (personal communication, September 4, 2015), explains: 'Purple is Löfbergs. Although the company has grown bigger by means of mergers and acquisitions and increased its share in the international market, the bonds to our history are still strong. The purple enables communication with the origin of the business, defining where we come from.'

The past also defines where to go. Göran Sonesson (personal communication, February 6, 2015) mentions the project 'The Purple Road to Success' with the aim to identify changes needed in different areas and ensure that we all are in the same boat, rowing in the same direction. Kathrine Löfberg (personal communication, June 9, 2015) refers to the 'Purple question'. Closely related to the sense of intention inculcated in the practitioners by the Löfbergs legacy, it concerns vision, strategy and goals for being the leader in good tasting coffee, sustainability and long-term profitability, and is translated into all functions and areas of the organization. 'Intention' gains a purple colour. In order to involve everyone, instilling a sense of purple intention, already the recruitment process communicates the Löfbergs legacy through the good-will values.

Involving Everyone

The recruitment process actively communicates the good-will values. Human Resourses Manager Helena Eriksson (personal communication, July 2, 2015) points out:

We are upfront about our five values and when interviewing potential employees we encourage them to describe their approach to the values. We explore how their understanding of the values aligns with ours. The prospective employee must carefully consider what it means to be employed and work in accordance with the values. Examples of questions asked are: What do you mean by responsibility? What do you think could be of importance in the long term? Even if there is no substantial difference between two candidates in terms of competence and our gut feeling is equally good for both, their understanding of our values might deviate.

Göran Sonesson (personal communication, February 6, 2015), adds: 'Yes, you get to know people already during the recruitment process . . . and in terms of values, at a very early stage in the recruitment process, you pick up pretty quickly on how the person in question fits with you.'

Sales Director Kent Pettersson (personal communication February3, 2015) tells:

We receive a large number of applications from people revealing that their dream at a very young age was to work at Löfbergs. To be hired by Löfbergs describes elated feelings of contentment . . . As newly recruited you feel very welcome and soon you become acquainted with everyone. This is something special. And you also realize that people are fully engaged in their work, feeling proud being associated with Löfbergs. I am not originally from Värmland, yet convinced that Löfbergs enjoys enormous respect and has a great reputation in the region; the name Löfberg is associated with unprecedented uniqueness.

Further, Helena Eriksson (personal communication, July 2, 2015) informs us:

All new starters are invited to an introductory training course where they receive a copy of Our Good Will book. At the very first lecture our CEO clarifies what the good will is about, carefully explaining what each value stands for . . . The good-will values and my feelings about what is right to do are a most important part of my reality and everyday work life . . . our values are deeply ingrained in our way of interacting.

Sharing this experience, Kent Pettersson (personal communication, February 3, 2015) asserts:

Our good will refers to transparency, fairness and honesty . . .We have no hidden agenda. We rely on, communicate and live our values . . . It is important to always reflect on what you say and how you approach and interact with people. You must also live the values in relation to people not directly associated with Löfbergs. Everywhere and every day, even on Saturdays and Sundays you are Löfbergs.

On the basis of the values, Pettersson has created an image of the good-will values. At monthly meetings with the sales team, the twenty-three members of the team are reminded of the values. The value image provides guidance for action and is used as a means to reduce and resolve conflicts.

Helena Eriksson (personal communication, April 20, 2012; July 2, 2015) adds:

Constantly we highlight the importance of bringing the values alive in our daily activity. In consolidating the values, Löfbergs-practitioners get reminded every so often of the values, for example, by pictures nailed to the wall, during kick-off days, at management training courses and in the recently launched Talent Program. This program is designed for personal development for both women and men and creates a long-term platform for empowering women to take up leadership positions. Moreover, value-based leadership criteria have been formulated. And I would like to add, our values are particularly helpful in conflict situations; they provide a starting point and a structure for a conversation about actions that do not align with the values and help to resolve conflicts. If you do not know how to begin the conversation, you should definitely rely on the values and use them as a tool. People out of alignment with our values are inclined to work towards goals with outcomes that make it difficult to implement our strategy and materialize our vision ... During the past years we have arranged a number of coaching sessions around a fictitious problem to which the managers are requested to apply the values. At meetings with the department heads, we make sure that they are able to explain the meaning of the five values and most importantly, live the values. Of course, the words used when translating the values to everyday practice vary. Depending on who you are as a person you attribute different roles to the values. For me, the value of responsibility is particularly close to my heart. Taking responsibility implies never leaving any loose ends; you finish what you have started. I think that is crucial. It is, in addition, important to state clearly when you are not supposed to be involved, pointing out that the responsibility is somebody else's. Our new organization, from 1 July 2015, is an example of how we define responsibility. Job descriptions have been provided, outlining each position's responsibilities.

In the capacity as Employee Representative of Unionen (the Swedish trade union), Supply Chain Administrator Charlotte Blomquist (personal communication, September 2, 2015) points out that the values also apply in her interactions with the members of the local Unionen organization. Negotiations on pay, working hours and working conditions are carried out on the basis of criteria that clearly link to the good-will values. In the capacity of Club Chairman of the Swedish Food Workers' Union, Process Operator Johan Eriksson (personal communication,

September 4, 2015) presents the value of responsibility as 'doubled': 'Of course, the responsibility I have towards the members and the company remains the same. It is a double responsibility that describes a symbiotic relationship . . . if the company prospers the members of the Union prosper.' Per Grahn (personal communication, February 25, 2015) associates the value of responsibility with keeping one's word, caring for and engaging in regional and local projects, underlining that responsibility is actualized between people, in their relationships and interactions:

> If we make a promise to the customer, fundamental is to carry out that promise, making sure that the customer is not deceived. Responsibility does also imply caring about and engaging in regional and local development projects in Karlstad in cooperation with other local actors. Examples are the shopping mall "Mitt i City", "Löfbergs Arena", mainly used for ice hockey and live music performance, and "CCC", Karlstad Congress and Culture Centre. There is no short-term acting and what we say, we do; we walk the talk. The family owns a real estate company that engages regionally and locally. Though not directly related to the coffee business, it builds on the very same values.

Responsibility is thus also exemplified through acting for the benefit of society. As Lars Appelqvist (personal communication, August 31, 2015) clarifies: 'The value of responsibility drives all other values. The values cannot be separated from each other; they constitute a web. In this web responsibility plays a prominent role.'

Constituting a Löfbergs World of Good-Willed Practising

The values of responsibility, commitment, long-term approach, entrepreneurship and professionalism are communicated to everyone. Not merely used as tools and a compass, the values existentially extend between members of different generations of the Löfberg family, and others, constituting a Löfbergs world of good-willed practising. As Göran Sonesson (personal communication, February 6, 2015) expresses it: 'Our good will goes back to the feeling of being part of this business, having a built-in sense of being very integral to what we do and for me this is most fundamental.' According to Anders Löfberg (personal communication, November 4, 2015) it is impossible to draw boundaries around company, family and coffee, marking out three units. A predefined three-unit structure cannot be imposed on the Löfbergs business. Anders Löfberg lives the business. This life incorporates the members of the owner family, but also others not related to the family by blood or included through marriage. They intrinsically entwine with a Löfbergs world of practising. This world is characterized by passion, indicates Kathrine Löfberg (personal communication, June 9, 2015): 'To me and many others, the passion for coffee is essential, it makes work and life intertwine ... One cannot draw a distinction between work and life; they fade into each other. It is not an ordinary job – you live it and Löfbergs is not merely a company. No.' Anna Nordström (personal communication, August 4, 2015) asserts: 'Löfbergs coffee, in particular, stands for passion.'

Living the good-will values, practitioners entwine with a Löfbergs world that gives them a sense of meaning. In reference to a meaningful Löfbergs life, Lars Appelquist (personal communication, August 31, 2015) discloses:

Two things make my Löfbergs life meaningful; it is very fun and exciting to be part of and be able to contribute to this business and for me, personally, it is enriching and stimulating and I feel very content. It is then not only about looking out for the interests of others but also for my own interest, which gives meaning and is a greater incentive than extra monetary compensation. There are other things that are more valuable than money. If all members of the management team expected a higher salary they would look for employment elsewhere ... Other, non-monetary things instill in me the right gut feeling both when I leave office in the evening and return the next morning and this feeling is worth a great deal to me.

Climate changes, exacerbating a range of risks to our planet, are important to consider when defining a meaningful Löfbergs life. According to Appelqvist (personal communication, March 31, 2014):

In recent years, sustainability has been of growing recognition and sustainability is now more tightly linked to our business. We actively integrate sustainability into our business model ... sustainability entails moral responsibility. We talk about different dimensions of sustainability and the need to maintain a balance between economic, environment, climate and social aspects of our business, fundamental to which is ethics as expressed by our values.

From the viewpoint of Sustainability Director Eva Eriksson (personal communication, February 13, 2015):

The meaning of my Löfbergs life adheres to my feeling of being able to contribute to the success of our business in a sustainable way. I prefer the expression: Business as usual is not an option, which builds on Professor Rockström's statement: "The planetary risks we are facing are so large that business as usual is not an option." Meaning denotes being able to run a business without impinging negatively on the life of the planet. I really sense that to be meaningful ... yet, all humans do not understand where we are heading if not seriously considering the planetary boundaries ... Last week I attended a meeting, listening to a presentation by Mikael Karlsson, for several years Chairman of the Swedish Society for Nature Conservation; he pointed to the immediate need to tackling climate changes; we need to act otherwise we are doomed.

The good-will values constitute a moral human agency that includes the aspect of sustainability. When looking towards a future, materializing the purple intention, Löfbergs-practitioners appear to be sensitive about a wider world of practising. 'We care very much about the natural world and the entire planet Earth, Anders Löfberg (personal communication, November 4, 2015) asserts.

Unfolding Moral Human Agency – Commentary (III)

As indicated in this section, practising, maintaining the good-will values in close relation to the purple intention, unfolds moral human agency in the iterational dimension. Löfbergs-practitioners reveal that throughout the past 110 years, the Löfberg family through each generation in inter-action with the employees has striven to make the world better by offering the customers and consumers a coffee that both tastes good and does good. In the deictic here and now, not distinguishing family members from non-family members, there is a 'we' entangled in an invisible past that nonlinearly affords a present–past–future relationality.

Not bound to the linearity of the value chain activities, the iterational dimension points to a belongingness to a Löfbergs world that draws in otherness in regard to a past. A past is brought alive at present by Anders Löfberg, owner, former CEO and Chairman of the Board of Directors, through the retelling of the Löfbergs history and the articulation and effectuation of the good-will values and adherent purple intention. Relational activity spaces are rewound at present, colourfully illustrating how the coffee business evolved with values 'passed on' and the 'Löfbergs legacy' kept alive across generations of the Löfberg family. However, the 'passing on' constitutes a stream of activities and processes through which people learn about how to do business (Haag 2012). This translates to a fusion of horizons. From a philosophical-hermeneutical viewpoint, learn-ing conjoins with 'horizon', which akin to 'situation' represents a stand-point and that which can be seen from that standpoint (Gadamer 1989).

By introducing the Gadamerian concept of horizon to the iterational dimension more clarity can be provided to the relations among present, past and future. A prior generation of the Löfberg family is rather a *horizon* that speaks of a past, represented and reactivated at present with a future in sight as pronounced through the 'Purple Road to Success' interlinked with the 'purple intention'. A past is not solidified into *the* past that Löfbergs-practitioners and other people look back on or paint a picture of and hang on the wall. 'If, *per impossible*, we were to reach that past event as it took place we should have to be in that event, and then compare it with what we now present as its history', Mead (1932: 74, emphasis in original) purports.

The iterational dimension also proposes a move beyond the notion of sustainability. As we travel a world of strategy practising, it is necessary in close relation to Ricoeur's (1992) 'ethical aim' to include moral-philosophical reflections for enriching our interpretation and understanding of moral human agency (cf. Franck 2014) being aware that we cannot restrict our focus to a level of morality where sustainability gains exclusivity. A focus on participation in human interaction in terms of betweenness makes us realize that morality is also about reciprocity, fellow-feeling, passion and meaning.

On the basis of the empirical-theoretical discussion, proceeding through the three sections of this chapter, our-good-will context of Löfbergs coffee emerges as moral human agency temporal-relationally unfolds in the projective, practical-evaluative and iterational dimensions. This will be further elaborated in the subsequent and final chapter, Chapter 6.

6   A Temporal-Relational Conceptualization of Moral Human Agency

By travelling a world of strategy practising through the aroma and taste of Löfbergs coffee, linearly describing value chain activities from bean to cup while nonlinearly attending to a past, we gain insight into moral human agency. The our-good-will context emerges (Chapter 5). By including the group context of Löfbergs coffee (Chapter 4), we recognize a need for a move away from a description of a given object to a context in the making. The group description serves as a sensitizing device, holding a forward movement that makes the predefined object dissolve in its contours. In musical terms, composed as a prelude it introduces succeeding themes of increased complexity that allow for our-good-will coffee context to fade in. In this context, the Löfbergs Group, the owner family and the coffee product are not separated by boundaries enforced through a thing-like representation and there is no subject–object relationship that identifies individuals as discrete units and categorizes them as family and non-family members.

We cannot deny the existence of a person as 'a flesh and blood sense-maker' (Van Manen 1990: 14) but in dialogical openness welcome the Other, extending beyond the particularity of either person alone through a focus on human betweenness. While maintaining a view of agency cultivated by a relational ontology, any attempt to encircle and attribute distinctiveness to a 'unit' is doomed to fail. An our-good-will reality is a relational reality that cannot be decomposed into simpler elements without destroying it (Christians 2003). As in a melody, units are played in resonance although not necessarily always striking a chord in harmony in the avoidance of dissonance. The melody dims every effort to convert and objectify the tones into tangible units to be studied from the outside.

Strategy practising constitutes bean-to-cup activities with which practitioners and other people entwine, uncovering morally imbued in-betweens. What is labelled the our-good-will context of Löfbergs coffee emerges as these in-betweens unfold projective, practical-evaluative and iterational dimensions. As pointed out in this chapter, the dimensions afford a temporal-relational conceptualization of moral human agency with morality associated with good as will and values. 'Good' puts teleological and deontological ethics in play in reference to a specified end and a duty but accounts also for justice in connection to reciprocity for mutual benefit and respect and a meaningful Löfbergs life that yields a morality almost unreflective in character, a felt direction. A temporal-relational conceptualization of moral human agency is presented as a supplement to the existing body of strategy-as-practice research. Also noted, the activity of supplementing implicates bridge-building among strategy-as-practice research, moral philosophy, business ethics and family business research. The Final Comment underlines that moral human agency in business is not confined to 'business'.

Unfolding Projective, Practical-Evaluative and Iterational Dimensions

From-bean-to-cup activities linearly describe a human agency that in the projective dimension allows for the generation of new ideas translated to future practising and in the practical-evaluative dimension proposes a move in a future direction that deviates from a past. As pointed out, human agency also extends through material arrangements in these dimensions (Commentary I and II, Chapter 5). From-bean-to-cup activities further disclose a human agency that unfolds the iterational dimension. Nonlinearly, the construction of a living relationship to a past and belongingness to a Löfbergs world of practising bring in the iterational dimension (Commentary III, Chapter 5).

Future-orientated environmental, social and financial concerns give relief to the projective dimension, which alludes to possibilities imagined and created among Löfbergs-practitioners, coffee farmers, representatives of International Coffee Partners (ICP), customers and consumers. Following Emirbayer and Mische (1998) the projective dimension accounts for anticipatory identification (Chapter 3). This entails continual re-evaluation of sustainability work with anticipatory identification represented through the vision of 'Good Moments for Future Generations' (Chapter 4). The vision supposedly serves as a temporal framing of value chain activities, encouraging the Löfbergs-practitioners in interaction with others to engage actively in development work along sustainable, profitable and competitive paths.

The projective dimension closely relates to the practical-evaluative dimension (Emirbayer and Mische 1998). Both dimensions are future-orientated, but the practical-evaluative dimension, as opposed to the projective, allows for normative judgement, which in response to challenges faced, needs and requirements raised among Löfbergs-practitioners and other people prompts a distancing from past ways of interacting. Communicatively, actors critically shape their responsiveness to problematic situations and distance themselves from old patterns, as Mead (1932) acknowledges. Löfbergs-practitioners in interaction with others respond to a number of challenges that allow for practical normative judgement. As illustrated (Chapter 5), challenges refer to the establishing of cooperatives in coffee producing countries, the empowerment of coffee farmers to operate on a long-term sustainable basis for improving productivity and livelihood, and the provision of better functioning infrastructure in remote and desolate locations, health care and education for the farmers' children. Moreover, challenges refer to unforeseen fluctuations in the price of raw coffee traded on the New York Stock Exchange and the London Stock Exchange, retail customers' move from decentralized to centralized purchasing which allows them to exert more pressure on prices in negotiations with Löfbergs-practitioners, a mature coffee market where expansion opportunities and increases in profitability are limited and where competitors are getting bigger, the need for competitive differentiation through enhanced focus on sustainability and the accounting for cultural differences in countries where subsidiaries are established. When referring to the 1990s, we recognize challenges imposed by the need to direct more attention to eco-friendly and organic production of coffee and the difficulties experienced by some Löfbergs-practitioners to communicate to the customers and consumers the advantages of buying certified coffee. Still today there is much concern about consumption of coffee with effort put into changing the habits of customers and consumers. To deal with the different challenges, Löfbergs-practitioners immerse themselves in activities that mobilize normative judgement.

Practical evaluation includes problematization and characterization of an ambiguous and unresolved situation, deliberation in dealing with the situation and a decision (Emirbayer and Mische 1998). Practical evaluation could too imply temporal improvisation through controlling intervals between events and actions, and political decision making if agents experience multiple possibilities of action and wish to test the limits of a situation (Chapter 3). Because of scant information regarding people's involvement in such activities, we can only describe practical normative judgement with reference to the use of certification criteria, operational controls of Fairtrade and EU Organic coffee, reviews and follow-ups of sustainability projects, streamlined transportation, energy-efficient processing, daily quality tests of coffee, product development that employs the lock model, and ISO systems and standards (Chapter 5). It can also be asserted (when moving beyond the Löfbergs Group level), for dealing with ambiguous situations in a practical-evaluative sense, Löfbergs-practitioners rely on policies for quality and food safety, sustainability, work environment, personnel and purchasing, and further, on the Code of Conduct, the business ethics policy, and laws and regulations prevailing in the coffee producing countries and in the countries where the subsidiaries are established and operate (Chapter 4 and 5).

The iterational dimension announces that the historical world is always there and that 'we are historical beings first, before we are observers (Betrachter) of history', as Carrr (1986: 4) posits. There is thus another Other in the sense of a historical past from which it is impossible to flee (Ricoeur 1984). This past is a moving horizon and not something gained access to and transmitted through layers of people in the chronology of time. As pointed out (Commentary III, Chapter 5), relational activity spaces constructed by previous generations of the Löfberg family are rewound at present with values 'passed on' to the present generation and the 'Löfbergs legacy' kept alive. But a prior generation of the Löfberg family is rather a *horizon* of a past that becomes fused with the horizon of a present with a future outlined by the 'Purple road to success' in connection to the 'Purple intention'. The horizon of a present is not an isolated horizon consisting of a fixed set of opinions and valuations, and the horizon of a past is not fore-grounded by the present as a fixed ground, Gadamer (1989) submits. The Purple intention addresses the question of why Löfbergs-practitioners in interaction with others are roasting coffee, and hence, calls on a past to be responded to at present for dealing with the question of where to go in an imaginative future. The purple colour holds everything together, according to Anders Löfberg (owner, former CEO and Chairman of the Board of Directors). So it can be argued that also horizon in its present-past-future temporal relationality is purple in colour.

The projective, practical-evaluative and iterational dimensions provide insights into the ways in which morality is articulated and activated between humans in linear and nonlinear flows of time. A temporal-relational conceptualization of moral human agency develops, disclosing value chain activities that projectively construct a future while, at the same time, practical-evaluatively engaging normative judgement and iteratively promoting a fusion of the horizons of a past and a present. It builds on a three-dimensional interpretation and understanding of moral human agency with agency entailing dialogical openness to the Other and morality inherent in a good that is constitutive of a will that extends through and is pervaded by the values of responsibility, commitment, long-term approach, entrepreneurship and professionalism.

Morality in Association with Good as Will and Values

The concept of value has been in use for more than a thousand years, yet a fully accepted definition is lacking (Goodenough and Gruter Cheney 2008). There are many linguistic forms for evaluation and differing moral-philosophical understandings of value (Orsi 2015). Generally, values are thought of as deeply seated commitments that guide individuals' actions and as enduring beliefs about what constitutes a preferable existence (Goodenough 2008; Zak 2008). 'It indicates what we consider a "better" way of living. So after having lived in society for centuries, we may come to realize that it is preferable to treat other people fairly rather than unfairly . . . We therefore come to value certain states of existence', clarify Painter-Morland and ten Bos (2011: 9).

Values, also described in terms of virtues, are difficult to define in the abstract why they have been identified by examples, but this too is a complicated task, according to Goodenough and Gruter Cheney (2008). By focusing on our-good-will context informative descriptions of values can be provided. The from-bean-to-cup activities speak to us about values, not merely as guides to activity, but as ubiquitous activity realities (cf. Zak 2008). The values of responsibility, commitment, long-term approach, entrepreneurship and professionalism are articulated and activated in between Löfbergs-practitioners, coffee farmers, ICP representatives, customers and consumers (Chapter 5).

With the focus on responsibility, Bevan and Werhane (2011: 53), referring to Levinas (1987), clarify that responsibility 'does not arise from some rationalization of (stakeholder) claim, but in the encounter with the Other and outside of the self.' Also Rhodes (2011: 151) points to Levinas's theorizing of the relationship with the Other, arguing that 'the other person is not just a thing that can be exploited for the purposes of one's own enjoyment or happiness, but as an Other who disrupts such a quest for exploitation.' In our-good-will context, the value of responsibility, not exploited for selfish enjoyment, is effectuated in between humans - in building a transparent value chain and in sustainability work. Notably, the value of responsibility does not only apply to the value chain of Löfbergs coffee but also to another producer's value chain. If a product is bought from another producer, a careful check is carried out to see whether the producer's value chain, from raw material to end product, meets sustainability-based criteria that align with the good-will values. The value of responsibility is activated through keeping one's word in interaction with customers and others and is closely related to the commitment value.

Generally, commitment describes the relationship between the employee and the organization (Vitell and Hidalgo 2006), accounting for the three components, affective, continuance and normative (Meyer and Allen 1991). The affective component is characterised by attachment to social relationships, the continuance component refers to cost-avoidance and the normative to an employee's obligation to remain with the organization. The concept of 'commitment escalation' is used to explain family members' emotional attachment to and strong identification with the family business and the members' inclination to keep running the business in the face of failing profitability (Chirico *et al.* 2017). Not coinciding with an organization or a family business, our-good-will context displays a commitment that suggests affective and normative moral involvement in sustainable development work. The passion for making good coffee and the intention, akin to the feeling of duty, to produce coffee that does good translate into affective and normative commitment. 'Values that have lost their affective elements become empty shells, fragments of intellectual tracts or phrases to which people pay lip service but do not need much in their choices', Etzioni (1988: 105) comments. Normative commitment implies moral involvement in a dutiful sense, clearly distinguished from instrumental motivation with activity determined by an evaluation of personals costs and benefits (Meyer and Parfyonova 2010). Normatively, commitment can be used to curb affective expressions or to legitimate them (Etzioni 1988).

In our-good-will context, responsibility, inextricable from commitment, is a prerequisite for a long-term sustainable, profitable and competitive business. In connection with sustainability, the value of long-term approach entails close and enduring relationships with the coffee farmers and a concern for future generations of coffee farmers, customers and employees. Through the establishment of the position of Sustainability Director there is enhanced focus on long-term sustainability work. The value of long-term approach is not only future-oriented but also past-oriented (Nevins, Bearden and Money 2007). Assumed by chronological time is a succession of generations of the Löfberg family involved in sustainability work for more than one hundred years. The year 1905 represents a starting point for the Löfbergs business.

Moreover, long-term approach makes us aware of the relationship between short- and long-term acting, interrelated with the value of entrepreneurship. Although there are circumstances that necessitate short-term calculations and decision making, the Löfbergs-practitioners seem not very inclined to let a short-term perspective control the long term as long as new business opportunities can be developed in the market. As witnessed, Anders Löfberg is unique in the way in which he deals with business matters, honouring a time frame that extends 30,

40 and even 50 years ahead. This uniqueness activates the value of entrepreneurship. From the literature on entrepreneurship we learn that entrepreneurship is an inherently recombinative and disequilibrative process (Chiles, Bluedorn and Gupta 2007) and that entrepreneurship, where not reduced to cognitive processes, is realized through social processes (Fletcher 2003, 2006; Hjorth and Steyaert 2004; Jones, Latham and Betta 2008). Through the introduction and use of the *entrepreneuring* concept (MacMillan 1986; Steyaert 2007) the processual character is enhanced. The focus shifts away from the individual entrepreneur as an atomistic entity equipped with a set of traits and behaviours (Apospori, Papalexandris and Galanaki 2005) to a relational human who shares in entrepreneurial activity, both separating from and joining with others. It is in such a relational activity space (as formed by our-good-will context) the uniqueness of Anders Löfberg can be understood, and in the light of past days, a relational space too emerges, allowing for the effectuation of the entrepreneurship value in connection to his father Åke.

Long-term responsibility is interlinked with commitment to give a little extra in everyday interaction, and through thinking creatively the value of entrepreneurship is activated. Entrepreneurship is not only about doing new things, but doing things differently and in the opposite direction to the competitors. The entrepreneurship value is also made salient in the planning, implementation and evaluation of product development projects that require extensive coordination among Löfbergs-practitioners representing different functions, departments, business areas and subsidiaries. The value of entrepreneurship is further exposed by the improvements made in the roasting machinery, the development of techniques for lowering the use of energy and the use of alternative energy sources and material. It is worth repeating that Löfbergs-practitioners were first in Sweden to remove the laminate with aluminium in the packaging of coffee, and further that the world's first large-scale testing facility of solar panels for heating and cooling has been built and that 100,000 bees live on the Löfbergs rooftop for contributing to pollination and a greener urban environment.

The value of professionalism is closely associated with the integrity of the owners and can be said to be 'surrounded' and constrained by the values of responsibility, commitment, long-term approach and entrepreneurship. In this way some normative order is provided, which requests the Löfbergs-practitioners to understand the meaning of acting professionally in encounters with customers and other people. Evetts (2003) discusses professionalism as value system which puts demands on professionals to be worthy of trust in their relations with clients and customers. The value system contributes normative order through which professionals gain authority and status. In relation to the Löfbergs-prac-titioners, a normative order implies moral direction for making them coffee specialists and ambassadors for Löfbergs coffee, aware of the importance of always living the values everywhere and every day. A moral direction is fostered through professional socialization in the work place (Evetts 2003). This occurs already in the recruitment process where presumptive Löfbergs-employees are exposed to the good-will values and is further intensified during the introduction of new employees and thereafter, on a regular basis at department meetings, during kick-off days, management training courses and education programmes. Everyone must be able to explain what the values mean to them, practically sustaining the values and understanding how to use them when dealing with tensions and conflicts. The values help to eliminate doings that do not align with them.

The value of professionalism is maintained by employment terms and performance criteria equally applied to all employees regardless of kinship ties and ownership in the business. There is no opportunity given to a son or daughter of Anders Löfberg to hide under his fatherly wings. A distance in parent-child relation is too reflected in the requirement of a son and daughter to spend five years working in another industry before involving in the Löfbergs coffee business. When acting as coffee specialists and ambassadors for Löfbergs coffee, living the good-will values everywhere and always in interactions with people, the value of professionalism exceeds a normative character, becoming descriptive of human betweenness.

Instrumental and Dutiful Use, Justice and Meaning The five values interrelate but could differ in intensity (cf. Hall 2003) depending on the situation that emerges from human in-betweens. In-betweens do also ascribe different 'functions' to the values. The projective and practical-evaluative dimensions allow for an instrumental use of the values as well as a normative use that judges the morality of human in-betweens based on duty. This implies a good that bears traces of teleological and deontological ethics, recognizable of an Aristotelian and a Kantian heritage. The Aristotelian teleological perspective specifies the end, covering *techne* with its emphasis on craftsmanship and practical work but accounts also for *phronesis* in terms of practical wisdom that helps people distinguish between what is just and unjust to do (Aristotle 2011). From the Kantian deontological perspective a good will is determined by duty and an action done from duty is based on a maxim that can be raised to the level of a universal law (Kant 1956) (Chapter 3).

In our-good-will context, the value chain activities define an end that is teleological and instrumental in character, referring to *techne*. When faced with different kinds of challenges, the Löfbergs-practitioners appear also to exercise *phronesis*. Practical wisdom is not a special ability attributed a single rational human agent; communicative in character (Emirbayer and Mische 1998) it extends in dialogical interplay between Löfbergs-practitioners, coffee farmers, ICP representatives, customers and consumers. We can credit the practitioners' interactions with practical wisdom, although not in connection to the Aristotelian criterion of *mesotēs*, which requires taking the middle path in the avoidance of extremes, but with respect to that which is well deliberated and brings about the good as pronounced by the values of responsibility, commitment, long-term approach, entrepreneurship and professionalism.

Duty seems to arise between the Löfbergs-practitioners and in their interactions with other people out of the will to do something good, not necessarily in line with the Kantian universal law, but in line with normative and practical judgements made by the help of the good-will values as a moral compass that provides direction and prescribes what one ought to do for maintaining and developing sustainability in conjunction with profitability and competitiveness. When accounting for both the deliberate aim of producing coffee and the obligation to do so, a relation can be established between an Aristotelian-inspired teleological perspective and a Kantian-inspired deontological perspective, insisting on the possibility to overcome a gap between 'is' and 'ought to'. For Ricoeur (1992), the term 'ethics' is reserved for the aim and the term 'morality' for the articulation of this aim. With ethics characterized by a teleological view and morality a deontological view, the deontological is subordinated to the teleological. This subordination makes the gap between description and prescription, 'is' and 'ought to', less unbridgeable, according to Ricoeur (1992). However, in our-good-will context the projective and practical-evaluative dimensions flow from the deictic here and now, arguably sharing a common present without being hierarchically arranged. The end, specified by coffee that tastes good, and the inherent obligation to produce coffee that does good seem to amalgamate a teleological good with a deontological good.

Further, the projective, practical-evaluative and iterational dimensions allow for justice to be added to human agency, interlinked with fairness (Rawls 1971) and reciprocity for mutual benefit and respect (Hartley 2014; Laursen and Hartup 2002). Cooperation arises because agents expect future material benefits from their actions (Fehr and Gächter 2000), yet a sufficient condition for social cooperation is mutual respect, according to Hartley (2014). Also noted, not always symmetrical in character, reciprocity could pertain to situations in which the contributions of the parties are compensatory or complementary. Reciprocity precludes the domination by one party and the promotion of self-interest, providing a basis for justice, Rawls (1971) asserts, and 'extends all the way to the commonality of "living together"', adds Ricoeur (1992: 183). As with the Golden Rule, when reciprocity comes into play, otherness is introduced in the mediating terms of treating others as one would like to be treated by those others (Ricoeur 1992). Referring to Smith (1976: 141) this means that we should 'view ourselves, not in the light in which our own selfish passions are apt to place us, but in the light in which any other citizen of the world views us.' Smith (1976) holds that we are capable of feeling with others as well as for ourselves. This implies empathy. Following the Golden Rule is by no means the basis of morality, which is rather empathy, Solomon (2008) comments.

Relationally responsive (Fletcher 2006, 2007; Weick 1979) and in the name of justice, the Löfbergs-practitioners orient to each other and other people. Cooperation among practitioners, coffee farmers and ICP representatives; their exchange of information and the opportunities created for learning from one another about how to provide for sustainable growing, transportation and processing of coffee beans, while generating monetary income, assume reciprocity in terms of mutual benefit and respect. Teamwork, coordination, integration, controls and follow-ups of activities that engage practitioners representing different functions, departments, business areas and subsidiaries reflect reciprocity that is based on respect among the involved parties create benefits concerned with sustainable development and product launchings for the satisfaction of customers and consumers.

A sense of justice is further maintained in respect for and responsiveness to differences in customer and consumer habits and various roles coffee plays in countries where Löfbergs-practitioners, associated with the subsidiaries, operate. By also caring for coming generations of coffee farmers, employees, customers and consumers, there is awareness of what is just to do with mutual benefits implied in prospering coffee plantations, good-willed employees, and satisfied customers and consumers. Further, there are strong indications that people enjoy working together. Terms such as 'genuine' and 'fair' characterize the owners in their relationship to the employees. This borders on interactional justice, an aspect which more recently has been added to the aspects of distributive and procedural justice, which deal with the regulation of the distribution of social and economic advantages across society, and the fairness of the processes by which decisions are made (Rawls 1971). The interactional aspect includes interpersonal and informational justice

(Cohen-Charash and Spector 2001; Rhodes 2011). Interpersonal justice is the degree to which people are treated fairly and with politeness, dignity and respect, and informational justice concerns people's explanations about why a procedure has been used in a certain way and why certain outcomes have been reached (Colquitt *et al.* 2001).

The relation between justice and happiness and the extent to which happiness is distributed in equal proportions in the avoidance of pain (Bentham 1988; Mill 1998) and the procedure for distribution of justice in terms of rights and duties, benefits and burdens among the involved parties (Rawls 1971), the our-good-will context does not explain. Thus it is of little relevance to apply a utilitarian perspective that accepts, as the foundation of morality, utility in reference to the Greatest Happiness Principle (Mill 1998) (Chapter 3). When centring the focus on human in-betweens, neither is it of particular interest to probe further into the deontological Rawlsian view of justice. Rawls (1971, 2000) is mainly interested in how justice relates to principles for just structuring of society (Rhodes 2011). With reference to Levinas (1991), Byers and Rhodes (2007) hold that we cannot rely solely on teleological and deontological approaches because they tend to violate the particularity of the Other. In relation to organized work, in the situation of a plurality of others, there must be room for face-to-face relations and as our-good-will context reveals – a meaningful life.

Echoed by the good-will values is a meaningful Löfbergs world of strategy practising. In the iterational dimension, moral human agency accounts for a morality not merely associated with an instrumental and a dutiful use but also with meaning. Practitioners intimately connect with a Löfbergs world and gives meaning to practising in reference to 'their Löfbergs life', making 'sensitivity' an integral part of morality. To ground the good as will and values in being (cf. Jonas 1984) is thus to realize the possibility of the making of a relational space in association with meaning (Ricoeur 1992). 'Sensitivity is being able to sense that something is happening, to sense the way you respond, the way other people respond, to sense the subtle differences and similarities ... So sensitivity involves the senses, and also something beyond', Bohm (2004: 46) admits. But we cannot know to what extent meaning is shared among Löfbergs-practitioners. In this study, only a few practitioners are included, describing a meaning of a Löfbergs life. If a meaning is being shared, then it flows among the practitioners and in their interactions with others, showing sensitivity to all nuances (Bohm 2004).

Our-good-will context indicates that by means of sympathy practitioners share their pleasures with others, extending a good will towards others through fellow-feeling (cf. Hutcheson 2007; Smith 1976) and even convey a passion about their work. For Kathrine Löfberg (owner, Chairman of the Board of Directors) and many others, the passion for coffee makes work and life fade into each other. The practitioners are inspired beyond instrumentality and duty. Like love, passion makes us tremble. When love is present 'then responsibility is inspirited beyond duty by the devotion of the person who learns to tremble for the fate of that which is both worthy of being loved and beloved', as Jonas (1984: 92) expressively formulates it.

Good as will and values incorporates meaning and passion, attributing to morality an almost unreflective character, holding a felt sense of direction. We should then not focus all our attention on what happens in a linguistic setting, Shotter (2006: 596) warns, since 'our sense of "feelings of tendency", of felt "sense of direction" occurring in the course of our already ongoing actions enabling us to anticipate our own next movement, clearly occurs in all our bodily activities.' In reference to practical coping as a form of non-deliberate acting (Tsoukas 2015) and practical consciousness (Giddens 1979), practitioners' knowledge exceeds what they are able to articulate on the basis of discursive consciousness. As with Buber (in Anderson and Cissna 1997), good is direction, not destination. The from-bean-to-cup activities, constituting good-willed strategy practising, speak to us about values as ubiquitous activity realities. These morality insights, informed by a being-in-the-world view, are important, in connection to a temporal-relational conceptualization, to give to the study of strategy as practice.

Supplementing Existing Strategy-as-Practice Research

Moral human agency is left largely untheorized in strategy-as-practice research. Extensive reviews (Golsorkhi *et al.* 2015; Jarzabkowski and Spee 2009; Vaara and Whittington 2012) reveal that agency, associated with role, identity and subjectivity, predominantly is a question of how the individual strategist behaves within a predefined organizational context or field. Scholars enrich our understanding of sensemaking, discourse and sociomaterial agency (Chapter 2) but disregard morality and an agency that is constituted of human betweenness. Neither is much interest directed to a context that forms and extends as a physical product dissolves into activities with which practitioners entwine. A micro-level agency is related to a macro level defined by institutionalized rules and resources. A duality-based relationship between agency and structure, corollary to the micro and macro duality, illustrates how performative and ostensive aspects interlink (Chapter 2). The individual strategist is equipped with certain agentic qualities and 'separated by a structure of invisible "walls"' (Chia and Rasche 2015: 44). The general thrust of strategy-as-practice research is '*ways in which strategy work is conducted in specific organizational settings*', summarize Golsorkhi *et al.* (2015: 6, emphasis in original).

Langley (2015) describes strategy-as-practice research as an eclectic domain of study, and despite a continuing stream of studies and the use of a multiplicity of theoretical perspectives and methodologies there is limited concern for meta-theoretical, ontological questions. Although practice-based research with its focus on strategy as something people do (Johnson, Melin and Whittington 2003) suggests a break with the traditional view of strategy as something firms have, a fundamental ontological shift has not yet taken place (Golshorki *et al.* 2015).Splitter and Seidl's (2015) analysis of ontologies and epistemologies elicits that many scholars adopt a scholastic view built on scientific rationality. A scholastic view implies a distance between research and practice (cf. Sandberg and Tsoukas 2011). Jarzabkowski and Spee (2009) identify two ontological dimensions: individual and aggregate; inside and outside the organization. Arguably, both these dimensions account for a scholastic view grounded in scientific rationality, intended to represent a scientific truth about human action with little notion of lived experience as an expression of *geisting* (Chapter 1). Ricoeur (2007: 12) explains: 'Scientific truth thinks of itself as true without any recourse to a criterion of morality ... Since Galileo and Newton, there is no other form of cognitive thought worthy of acceding in the status of science other than one that passes through the formation of hypotheses ... .' A (scholastic) scientific truth originates in an objective ontology and a methodological individualism, which 'presumes that every individual is a discrete, bounded entity' that operates in a pre-established organizational setting (Chia and MacKay 2007: 219). This reminds us of a Cartesian split between the mental and the physical realms and of two Aristotelian forms of knowledge, namely,*episteme* and *techne* (Chia and Rasche 2015). *Episteme* represents a context-independent, rationality-based and objective truth, and *techne* stands for craftsmanship and practical instructions that can be explained verbally, clarify Chia and Rasche (2015).

The temporal-relational conceptualization of moral human agency pronounces a concern for practitioners' existential entwinement with a world of strategy practising. It proposes a move beyond institutional and organizational levels as well as a questioning of the predominance of the micro-macro contextualization translated into the language of agency and structure with the practitioner conceived of as a discrete thinking and acting agent. The two-category language and adherent Cartesian split are building blocks of a modernistic project, the image of which is

based on objective science and on ethics and morality as objective realities (Chan and Garrick 2002; Weiskopf and Willmott 2013). By adding
a temporal-relational conceptualization of moral human agency to the
study of strategy-as-practice research, the opportunity arises to go
beyond this 'language' and the Cartesian split. The notion of temporal
relationality dims the light on a bifurcation of agency and structure,
micro and macro. It prompts a re-composition of past experience and
encourages improvization and creation of innovative future trajectories
of actions and adjustment of norms developed in a past to changed
lived situations in a present (Emirbayer and Mische 1998). Although
a past might provide human in-betweens with relatively reliable knowledge of social relationship, structured through habit that helps to
sustain expectations about stability and continuity of activity, habit is
not devoid of agency (Camic 1986); the horizon of a present is continually in the process of being formed as it is also fused with the horizon of a
past (Gadamer 1989). This constructs temporally shifting contexts
for human agency to express morality in association with good as will
and values.

The temporal-relational conceptualization walks us on linear and nonlinear paths of time, promoting a focus on *practising* rather than *practice*.
As in French, it is more common to use the verb 'to practise' (*pratiquer*)
than the substantive form 'practice' used in English (Ricoeur 1992).
Temporal relationality is inherent in practising as in a fluid and open-
ended process (Tsoukas and Chia 2002) that constitutes a variety of
strategically oriented activities with which practitioners entwine, opening
up to a moral agency expressed through human betweenness. Otherness
implied in human betweenness invests with morality in association with
the good-will values of responsibility, commitment, a long-term
approach, entrepreneurship and professionalism.

On the basis of the discussions in this chapter of the projective,
practical-evaluative and iterational dimensions, and morality in association with good as will and values, we realize that the temporal-
relational conceptualization cultivates a good that brings teleological
and deontological ethics into play in reference to an instrumental and
a dutiful use of values and that promotes justice in connection to
reciprocity for mutual benefit and respect. Clearly, this is a justice that
in reference to betweenness emphasizes the interpersonal as a living
reciprocity and a willingness to meet with others openly with no intention to dominate (cf. Buber in Anderson and Cissna 1997). It is in an
expressive-responsive relation with the Other that justice is promoted, as
sympathy in association with a fellow-feeling. The temporal-relational
conceptualization further allows for a fusion of the horizon of a past with

the horizon of a present with implied meaning and passion adding a felt sense of direction to human agency.

In addition, in supplement to existing strategy-as-practice research, the temporal-relational conceptualization permits dialogical openness to other works and research in the encouragement of bridge-building. It bridges moral philosophical work and business ethics research and provides also a bridgehead to family business research. By opening up for a dialogue with business ethics scholars, there is potential for re-moralizing strategy. Once, strategy and ethics were interlinked (Chapter 2). Against the darkness of immoral acting in the business world, a renewal of strategy-ethics links is urgent, but this, with a focus on moral human agency in business – in the account of betweenness. Albeit the focus on morally imbued in-betweens is not limited to what occurs within the boundaries of a family firm (Chapter 1), it is nevertheless important also to broaden the discussion of strategy practising by linking to the study of family business.

Supplementing Implies Bridge-Building

By bridging moral philosophical work we are reminded that the Greek philosophical tradition and its inheritors exhibited strong interest in ethics and morality and that strategy-as-practice research can benefit from addressing this interest (Chapter 3). In connection to the dwelling worldview, Aristotle's (2011) concept of practical wisdom (*phronesis*) adds to our understanding of moral human agency. As Chia and Rasche (2015: 45, emphasis in original) acknowledge: 'Unlike *episteme* and *techne*, in which it is possible to make a distinction between intention and behavior, and hence between what one *is* and what one *does*, in *phronesis* what one *does* is inextricable from what one *is*.' 'Far from being individual or monological in nature, practical wisdom is intrinsically communicative in nature. It remains open to dialogue and persuasion and is profoundly implicated in common values, interests, and purposes', highlight Emirbayer and Mische (1998: 995). Hutcheson (2007) and Smith (1976) further raise our concerns about a morality that builds on social interactive qualities. Less focused on the rational (Descartes 1968) punctual self (Locke 2008), both Hutcheson (2007) and Smith (1976) hold that morality concerns what occurs between human beings (Chapter 3).

As Balogun, Beech and Johnson (2015) emphasize, moral and ethical reflection is needed in the area of strategy-as-practice research. Not only is an essential task then to bridge moral philosophical work but also business ethics research. Elms *et al.* (2010) urge practice scholars to explore how morality becomes operative in practice. With reference to Clegg, Kornberger and Rhodes (2007) they suggest a focus on business ethics as practice and an examination of how ethics are embedded in practice. Strategy-as-practice scholars are advised to explore the role social and moral norms play in business practices, overcoming the problem of 'scientific naïveté'. Citing Donaldson (2003), Clegg, Kornberger and Rhodes (2007: 107) accentuate that 'one problem preventing us from taking ethics more seriously is a form of scientific naïveté where we regard ethics as worse than "soft" because it lacks a theoretical foundation.'

In order to take ethics more seriously, strategy-as-practice studies could be more explicit about a philosophical-theoretical foundation, acknowledging the more recent developments in the study of business ethics that build on works of Foucault (2001), Ricoeur (1992, 2007) and Levinas (1987), for example. Although practice scholars use a Foucauldian approach they seem to be rather negligent of Foucault's ethical theorizing. For Foucault (2001), the discursive architecture through which we understand the world includes ethical positioning (Ibarra-Colado *et al.* 2006). Researchers need then to examine 'what ethics are politically constructed in what ways in organizations and how certain sorts of behaviour are enacted and constituted as (un)ethical social actions by practices of the organization, its management, its employees and the broader community' (Clegg, Kornberger and Rhodes 2007: 118). With Foucault (e.g. 2001), we can see ethics as emerging in relation to discursively constituted norms that are institutionally inscribed in organizational power-knowledge technologies (Chan and Garrick 2002; Loacker and Muhr 2009).

With regard to *parrhesia* (the Foucauldian term translated as 'fearless speech') there is no self-contained individual but a social self, who in relation to the Other is able to demand responsibility of the Other and interrupt the reproduction of institutionalized practices (Weiskopf and Willmott 2013).'Self' is a discursive conception of social agency (Laine and Vaara 2007, 2015) and denotes a 'work-in-progress' subjectivity (Allard-Poesi 2015: 243), clearly differentiated from subjectivity as an independent self. This agent thus forms in relation to and in communication with others, which is important to consider for furthering our understanding of agency in connection with morality, as elevated through the temporal-relational conceptualization.

In relation to business ethics, Rhodes, Pullen and Clegg (2010) examined an organization's capacity for ethical deliberation. Drawing on Ricoeur (1984) they show how stories about downsizing in a multinational information technology company became dominated by a narrative that focused more on securing the company's instrumental goals than on ethics. Although Ricoeur (1984, 1991) also plays an important role for De La Ville and Mounoud's (2015) outline of a research agenda for a narrative approach to strategy as practice research, a discussion of ethics is missing. They appear to be more interested in highlighting the mediating role of strategic text between institutional contexts that dominate and inform the strategic text and the organizational members' reading of the text as a process of consumption and comprehension.

Inspirational for bridge-building between strategy-as-practice research and business ethics research is Byers and Rhodes's (2007) study in which Levinas's (e.g.1991) thinking is applied to ethics and justice in organizations. From their perspective, organizational actions grounded in ethics seek legitimization primarily from welcoming the Other. The ethical integrity of an organization cannot be secured only by justice based on rules and principles in response to a legal requirement externally imposed by an institutional context. Levinas's conceptualization of the Other points in another direction. Byers and Rhodes (2007: 249) contend: 'Hence, while justice requires rules and principles, they must always be rendered, by me, before the Other in proximity, face to face, in a relation of honour.' Ethics is an encounter with the Other (Jeanes and Muhr 2010). In the context of the Other it would also be of interest to reflect on how Levinas's (1987) phenomenology relates to Ricoeur's (1992) phenomenology of the Other, moving to the fore the problematic of same and selfhood in relation to self, and reciprocity in relation to responsibility.

In Relation to Family Business Research The present study provides additional opportunity for discussing strategy in relation to family business research in consideration of values, roles, arenas and legitimacy. Family business scholars have already opened up to a dialogical interplay between strategy-as-practice research and family business research (Hall 2003; Nordqvist 2005; Hall, Melin and Nordqvist 2006). As Nordqvist (2011)indicates, strategy-as-practice research introduces concepts and research methods originating in sociology that can contribute to a better understanding of how strategy processes unfold in a family business. Strategizing with its focus on detailed processes, day-to-day activities and human involvement is highly relevant for the context of family business. Hall, Melin and Nordqvist (2006) contribute four perspectives of strategizing: values, role, arena and legitimacy.

The values perspective accounts for the special logic provided by the core values of the family. These are described as social principles, ethical and moral codes that in addition to profit making underpin human action and influence the delineation of the organization's final goals. The role perspective acknowledges the overlapping roles of family member, owner and business manager. Through the enactment of roles, individuals create their identities. The arena perspective points to a strategizing that takes place in different formal and informal arenas that offer opportunities for dialogues and communication on strategic issues. The legitimacy perspective enhances stability and conformability of organizational activities. In relation to family firms, legitimacy is often searched for through the spread and translation of ideas and best practises, Hall, Melin and Nordqvist (2006) note.

In connection to the strategizing perspective of values, the ethical dimension can be made more salient. As Adams, Taschian and Shore (1996) point out, there has not been much research on ethics in family business. It was not until recently that studies have come to show an interest in the ethical dimension (e.g. Blombäck and Wigren 2008; Blombäck and Wigren-Kristoferson 2014) in regard also to philanthropic activities (Campopiano, De Massis and Chirico 2014). It is important to bridge these studies when furthering our understanding of moral human agency and in relation to moral values discussing family values (Blombäck, Brunninge and Melander 2011) as well as other forms of socio-emotional wealth. Such a discussion could also account for the ability to exercise authority (Schulze, Lubatkin and Dino 2003), conservation of social capital (Arregle et al. 2007), fulfillments of family obligations based on blood ties (Athanassiou et al. 2002), emotional values (Zellwegger and Astrachan 2008) and with a focus on transgenerational transfer of practices direct attention to moral emotions of compassion (Akhter, Brundin and Härtel 2016). Since there are indications that entrepreneurship and family business studies are moving closer to each other (e.g. Akhter 2016; Chirico and Nordqvist 2010; Nordqvist, Habbershon and Melin 2008; Nordqvist and Melin 2010) there is also a possibility to gain deeper insight into the value of entrepreneurship as an integral part of a web of values that activities effectuate.

In terms of a citation analysis of family business articles published in leading family business and entrepreneurship journals for the period of 2003 to 2008, Chrisman et al. (2010) identified works that have shaped the state of the art in the field of family business. Their analysis suggests that to progress, family business studies should focus on how conflict and consensus emerge, how family relationships affect the performance of the business, a family's involvement as a source of entrepreneurial opportunity and the development of a theoretical definition of family business. Agency theory and the resource-based view are regarded as useful for explaining what family firms do. Effort should also be put into rich theory-based conceptualization of various phenomena, argues Sharma (2006). Qualitative research grounded in a relational ontology could then be of interest, inspiring enhanced focus on human betweenness and morality in association with good as will and values. As the current study is very limited in its empirical focus, future studies of moral practising need to include many other practitioners, who in relational responsiveness to each other and other people construct good-will contexts.

A Final Comment

The temporal-relational conceptualization is constituted of human in-betweens, allowing for a moral agency that in the construction of a good-will context expresses and effectuates values in a way that exceeds duality-based moral explanations. In moral philosophical work, good is often contrasted with evil, conjoined with other dualisms such as just and unjust (Plato 2000; Aristotle 2011), certainty and uncertainty (Descartes 1968), pleasure and pain (Locke 2008; Bentham 1988; Mill 1998), the hands of nature and the hands of man (Rousseau 2003), joy and sorrow (Hutcheson 2007), decent and indecent passions (Smith 1976) (Chapter 3). These provide a binary moral guide for action which implicates a will to do the right thing. '*Will* in moral philosophy is the capacity or power of making deliberate choices regarding one's actions, and thereby guiding one's actions by means of thought. And as a first approximation such will is free when it follows the agent's own wishes rather than being constrained or manipulated', summarizes Rescher (2009: 16, emphasis in original). Consistent with Cartesian ethics, which splits thinking and acting, mind and body, the power of will is the individual's own rational ability to affirm or deny, to pursue or flee a thing (Descartes 1968).

Our-good-will context is less concerned with a two-poled morality and a free will, disclosing a good that is multidimensional in character because good stands in a relation to a will that extends through the values of responsibility, commitment, long-term approach, entrepreneurship and professionalism and becomes pervaded by these values. A free will based on an individual's own deliberate choices, wishes and rational control cannot be discerned when the focus centres on human in-betweens. Morality in association with good as will and values concerns how human beings relate to each other (Taylor 1989), in the passage from the ethical aim to morality prompting a dialogic structure that incorporates otherness (Ricoeur 1992). Irreducible to a good as one pole of a duality, the temporal-relational conceptualization transcends a polarity expressed through a duality-based understanding of morality.

The relational-ontological interpretation, understanding and application (Chapter 1) pursued in this book contrast with *analysis*, which rather reflects a scholastic view assuming a distance between the investigator and the investigated, the subject and object. Of course there could be a distance from the Other and difficulties in accessing the Other's lived experience (Van Manen 1990). We must be aware that we can only understand fragments of lived experience (Schutz 1967) and that it is difficult to grasp felt ways of orienting and coping (Shotter 2006). Still, it is important to make an effort in a relational-ontological direction, enforcing the view that morality is 'rooted in the very way we are human' (Chan and Garrick 2002: 693). It is important to acknowledge that we continuously join with the Other and therefore should try to avoid 'the hazards of rigidifying aspects of agency' (Somers 1994: 606).

Relational ontologically, moral human agency is an aspect of *geisting*. Then we cannot rely on a scholastic view and in the defence of an objective ontology and adherent methodological individualism validate as the only truth that which the group context of Löfbergs coffee informs us about based solely on an 'analysis' of business ethics in integration with CSR, stakeholders and sustainability. The temporal-relational conceptualization adds to strategy-as-practice research a *lived* truth about moral human agency in business. This truth moves practice and theory more closely together as it tells us about that which occurs between practitioners as moral beings intrinsically involved in a Löfbergs world of strategy practising, not confined within the boundaries of an organization.

An interpretation, understanding and application, focused on strategy as practising with a concern for moral human agency, allows for dialogical encounters with the Other as human and, in addition, with a past (Commentary III, Chapter 5) and nature. Human in-betweens are mediated by nature in relation to geographical place, coffee plantation, harvest, soil, rain and drought, for example (Chapter 4). An encounter with this particular Other proposes enlarging the horizon from which we speak about and live morality. Löfbergs-practitioners and other people entwine with from-bean-to-cup activities that consider a future and a past of human and of nature. Arguably, the temporal-relational conceptualization reflects a *Löfbergian* ethics which translates into a good-willed practising that also makes biospheric concerns an integral part of a Löfbergs life. Anthropocentric confinement does not hold (Jonas 1984) as moral human agency in business is not strictly confined to 'business'; the missing dimension in strategy-as-practice impressionistically extends in time and space.

References

Adams, J. S., Taschian, A., and Shore, T. H. (1996). 'Ethics in family and non-family owned firms: An exploratory study', *Family Business Review*, 9/2: 157–70.

Adger, W. N. (2003), 'Social capital, collective action, and adaptation to climate change', *Economic Geography*, 79/4: 387–404

Adger, W. N., and Brown, K. (2010), 'Progress in global environmental change', *Global Environmental Change*, 20: 547–49.

Adler, P. S., and Kwon, S-W. (2002), 'Social capital: Prospects for a new concept', *Academy of Management Review*, 27/1: 17–40.

Aggerholm, H. K., Asmuβ, B., and Thomsen, C. (2012), 'The role of contextualization in the multivocal, ambiguous process of strategizing', *Journal of Management Inquiry*, 21/4: 413–28.

Aguinis, H., and Glavas, A. (2012), 'What we know and don't know about corporate social responsibility: A review and research agenda', *Journal of Management*, 38/4: 932–68.

Ahuja, G. (2000), 'Collaboration networks, structural holes, and innovation: A longitudinal study', *Administrative Science Quarterly*, 45/3: 425–55.

Akhter, N. (2016), *Family Business Portfolios: Enduring Entrepreneurship and Exit Strategies*. Doctoral dissertation. Jönköping, Sweden: Jönköping International Business School.

Akhter, N., Brundin, E., and Härtel, C. (2016), 'Transgenerational moral emotions: Activation compassion to develop a positive organization', in Akhter, N., *Family Business Portfolios: Enduring Entrepreneurship and Exit Strategies*, 189–230. Doctoral dissertation. Jönköping, Sweden: Jönköping International Business School.

Alexander, J., (1988), *Action and Its Environments*. New York, NY: Columbia University Press.

Allard-Poesi, F. (2015), 'A Foucauldian perspective on strategic practice: Strategy as the art of (un)folding', in Golsorkhi, D., Rouleau, L., Seidl, D., and Vaara, E. (eds.), *Cambridge Handbook of Strategy as Practice*, 78–94. Cambridge: Cambridge University Press.

Alvesson, M., and Kärreman, D. (2011), 'Decolonizing discourse: Critical reflections on organizational discourse analysis', *Human Relations*, 64/9: 1121–46.

(2007), 'Constructing mystery: Empirical matters in theory development', *Academy of Management Review*, 32/4: 1265–81.

(2000), 'Taking the linguistic turn in organizational research: Challenges, response, consequences', *The Journal of Applied Behavioral Science*, 36/2: 136–58.

Alvesson, M., and Willmott, H. (1996), *Making Sense of Management: A Critical Introduction*, London: Sage.

Anderson, R., and Cissna, K. N. (1997), *The Martin Buber – Carl Rogers Dialogue: A New Transcript with Commentary*. Albany, NY: SUNY Press.

Andrew, K. (1971), *The Concept of Corporate Strategy*, Homewood, IL: Dow-Jones Irwin.

Annual Report with Sustainability Report, 2013/2014; 2014/2015. Karlstad, Sweden: AB Anders Löfberg.

Apospori, W., Papalexandris, N., and Galanaki, E. (2005), 'Entrepreneurial and professional CEOs: Differences in motive and responsibility profile', *Leadership & Organization Development Journal*, 26/2:141–62.

Aristotle (2011), *Nicomachean Ethics*. Chicago: The University of Chicago Press.

Arregle, J-L., Hitt, M. A., Sirmon, D. G., and Very, P. (2007), 'The development of organizational social capital: Attributes of family firms', *Journal of Management Studies*, 44/1: 73–95.

Arrow, K. (1974), *The Limits of Organization*, New York, NY: Norton.

Athanassiou, N., Crittenden, W. F., Kelly, L. M., and Marquez, P. (2002), 'Founder centrality effects of Mexican family firms top management group: Firm culture strategic vision and goals, and firm performance', *Journal of World Business*, 37/2: 139–50.

Ayios, A., Jeurissen, R., Manning, P., and Spence, L. J. (2014), 'Social capital: A review form an ethics perspective', *Business Ethics*, 23/1:108–24.

Bakhtin, M. M. (1984), *Problems of Dostoevsky's Poetics*. Minneapolis: University of Minnesota Press.

(1981), *The Dialogical Imagination: Four Essays*. Austin: University of Texas Press.

Balmer, J. M. T., Fukukawa, K., and Gray, E. R. (2007), 'The nature and management of ethical corporate identity: A commentary on corporate identity, corporate social responsibility and ethics', *Journal of Business Ethics*, 76/1: 7–15.

Balogun, J., Beech, N., and Johnson, P. (2015), 'Researching strategists and their identity in practice: "Building close-with" relationships', in Golsorkhi, D., Rouleau, L., Seidl, D., and Vaara, E. (eds.), *Cambridge Handbook of Strategy as Practice*, 447–61. Cambridge: Cambridge University Press.

Balogun, J., Jacobs, C. D., Jarzabkowski, P., Mantere, S., and Vaara, E. (2014), 'Placing strategy discourse in context: Sociomateriality, sensemaking, and power', *Journal of Management Studies*, 51/2: 175–201.

Barnard, C. (1938), *The Functions of the Executives*. Cambridge, MA: Harvard University Press.

Bauman, Z. (1993), *Postmodern Ethics*. Oxford: Blackwell.

Beech, N., and Johnson, P. (2005), 'Discourses of disrupted identities in the practice of strategic change: The mayor, the street-fighter and the insider-out', *Journal of Organizational Change Management*, 18/1: 31–47.

Bentham, J. (1988), *The Principles of Morals and Legislation*. New York, NY: Prometheus Books.

Berger, L. P., and Luckmann, T. (1966), *The Social Construction of Reality*, Harmondsworth, UK: Penguin.

Berrone, P., Surroca, J., and Tribo, J. A. (2007), 'Corporate ethical identity as determinant of firm performance: A test of the mediating role of stakeholder satisfaction', *Journal of Business Ethics*, 76/1: 35–53.

Bevan, D., and Werhane, P. (2011), 'Stakeholder theory', in Painter-Morland, M., and ten Bos, R. (eds.), *Business Ethics and Continental Philosophy*, 37–60. Cambridge: Cambridge University Press.

Bhaskar, R. (1989), *Reclaiming Reality: A Critical Realist Introduction to Contemporary Philosophy*. London: Verso.

Bird, B., Welsch, H., Astracha, J. H., and Pistrul, D. (2002), 'Family business research: The evolution of an academic field', *Family Business Review*, 15/4: 337–50.

Blom, M., and Alvesson, M. (2015), 'A critical perspective on strategy as practice', in Golsorkhi, D., Rouleau, L., Seidl, D., and Vaara, E. (eds.), *Cambridge Handbook of Strategy as Practice*, 405–27. Cambridge: Cambridge University Press.

Blombäck, A., and Scandelius, C. (2013), 'Corporate heritage in CSR communication: A means to responsible brand image?', *Corporate Communications: An International Journal*, 18/3: 362–82.

Blombäck, A., and Wigren, C. (2008), 'Challenging the importance of size as determinant for CSR activities', *Management of Environmental Quality: An International Journal*, 20/3: 255–70.

Blombäck, A., and Wigren-Kristoferson, C. (2014), 'Corporate community responsibility as an outcome of individual embeddedness', *Social Responsibility Journal*, 10/2: 297–315.

Blombäck, A., Brunninge, O., and Melander, A. (2011), 'Corporate value statements – a means for family-controlled firms to monitor the agent?', *JIBS Working Papers No. 2011–14*. Jönköping, Sweden: Jönköping International Business School.

Bohm, D. (2004), *On Dialogue*. London and New York, NY: Routledge.

Boje, D. M. (2001), *Narrative Methods for Organizational and Communication Research*. London: Sage.

Bourdieu, P. (1990), *The Logic of Practice*. Cambridge: Polity.

Bowen, H. R. (1953), *Social Responsibilities of the Businessman*. New York, NY: Harper & Row.

Bowie, N. E. (2000), 'Business ethics, philosophy, and the next 25 years', *Business Ethics Quarterly*, 10/1:7–20.

Brammer, S., Jackson, G., and Matten, D. (2012), 'Corporate social responsibility and institutional theory: New perspectives on private governance', *Socio-Economic Review*, 10: 3–28.

Brewer, M. B., and Gardner, W. L. (1996), 'Who is this "We"? Levels of collective identity and self representations', *Journal of Personality and Social Psychology*, 71/1: 83–93.

Brown, A. D., Humphreys, M., and Gurney, P. M. (2005), 'Narrative, identity and change: A case study of Laskarina Holidays', *Journal of Organizational Change Management*, 18/4: 312–26.

Brundin, E., and Liu, F. (2015), 'The role of emotions in strategizing', in Golsorkhi, D., Rouleau, L., Seidl, D., and Vaara, E. (eds.), *Cambridge Handbook of Strategy as Practice*, 632–46. Cambridge: Cambridge University Press.

Brundin, E., and Nordqvist, M. (2008), 'Beyond facts and figures: The role of emotions in boardroom dynamics'. *Corporate Governance*, 16/4: 326–41.

Brundtland Report (1987) World Commission on Environment and Development: Common Future. Retrieved 2015-10-18, from www.un-documents.net/our-common-future.pdf.

Brytting, T. (1994), 'Moral support structures in Swedish Industry', in De Geer, H. (ed.), *Business Ethics in Progress?*, 70–87. Berlin/New York, NY: Springer-Verlag.

Burt, R. (1992), *Structural Holes: The Social Structure of Competition*. Cambridge, MA: Harvard University Press.

Business Ethics Policy for the Löfbergs Group (2014), Retrieved 2016-11-10, from www.lofbergs.se/wp-content/uploads/2015/12/business-ethics-policy-version-1.pdf

Byers, D., and Rhodes, C. (2007), 'Ethics, alterity, and organizational justice', *Business Ethics*, 16/3: 239–50.

Bygrave, W., and Minniti, M. (2000), 'The social dynamics of entrepreneurship', *Entrepreneurship Theory and Practice*, 24/3: 25–36.

Çalişkan, K., and Callon, M. (2010), 'Economization. Part 2: A research programme for the study of markets', *Economy and Society*, 39/1: 1–32.

Cambell-Hunt, C. (2007), 'Complexity in practice', *Human Relations*, 60/5: 793–823.

Camic, C. (1986), 'The matter of habit', *American Journal of Sociology*, 91:1039–87.

Campopiano, G., De Massis, A., and Chirico, F. (2014), 'Firm philanthropy in small and medium-sized family firms: The effects of family involvement in ownership and management', *Family Business Review*, 27/3: 244–58.

Carbon Trade Watch (2016). Retrieved 2016-11-10, from www.carbontradewatch.org/issues/monoculture.html

Carr, D. (1986), *Time, Narrative, and History*. Indianapolis: Indiana University Press.

Carroll, A. B. (2000), 'Ethical challenges for business in the new millennium: Corporate social responsibility and models of management morality', *Business Ethics Quarterly*, 10/1: 33–42.

(1991), 'The pyramid of corporate social responsibility: Toward the moral management of organizational stakeholder', *Business Horizons*, 34/4: 39–48.

(1979), 'A three-dimensional conceptual model of corporate performance', *Academy of Management Review*, 4/4: 497–505.

Chan, A., and Garrick, J. (2002), 'Organization theory in turbulent times: The traces of Foucault's ethics', *Organization*, 9/4: 683–701.

Chan, K. C., Fung, H-G., and Yau, J. (2013), 'Predominant sources and contributors of influential business ethics research: Evidence and implications from a threshold citation analysis', *Business Ethics: A European Review*, 22/3: 263–76.

Chapman, C. S., Chua, W. F., and Mahama, H. (2015), 'Actor-network theory and strategy as practice', in Golsorkhi, D., Rouleau, L., Seidl, D., and Vaara, E. (eds.), *Cambridge Handbook of Strategy as Practice*, 265–80. Cambridge: Cambridge University Press.

Chen, C-P., and Lai, C-T. (2014), 'To blow or not to blow the whistle: The effects of potential harm, social pressure and organisational commitment on whistleblowing intention behaviour', *Business Ethics: A European Review*, 23/3: 327–42.

Chia, R. (2004), 'Strategy-as-practice: Reflections on the research agenda', *European Management Review*, 1: 29–34.

Chia, R., and Holt, R. (2006), 'Strategy as practical coping: A Heideggerian perspective', *Organization Studies*, 27: 635–55.

Chia, R., and MacKay, B. (2007), 'Post-processual challenges for the emerging strategy-as-practice perspective: Discovering strategy in the logic of practice', *Human Relations*, 60/1: 217–42.

Chia, R., and Rasche, A. (2015), 'Epistemological alternatives for researching strategy as practice: Building and dwelling worldviews', in Golsorkhi, D., Rouleau, L., Seidl, D., and Vaara, E. (eds.), *Cambridge Handbook of Strategy as Practice*, 44–57. Cambridge: Cambridge University Press.

Chiles, T. H., Bluedorn, A. C., and Gupta, V. K. (2007), 'Beyond creative destruction and entrepreneurial discovery: A radical Austrian approach to entrepreneurship', *Organization Studies*, 28/4: 467–93.

Chirico, F., and Nordqvist, M. (2010), 'Dynamic capabilities and trans-generational values creation in family firms: The role of organizational culture', *International Small Business Journal*, 28/5: 487–504.

Chirico, F., Salvato, C., Byrne, B. M., Akther, N., and Múzquiz, J. A. (2017), 'Commitment escalation to a failing family business', *Journal of Small Business Management, online* 27 February.

Chrisman, J. J., Kellermanns, F. W., Chan, K. C., and Linao, K. (2010), 'Intellectual foundations of current research in family business: An identification and review of 25 influential articles', *Family Business Review*, 23/1: 9–26.

Christians, C. (2003), 'Ethics and politics in qualitative research', in Denzin, N., and Lincoln, Y. (eds.), *The Landscape of Qualitative Research*, 208–43. New York, NY: Sage.

Clarke, I., Kwon, W., and Wodak, R. (2012), 'A context-sensitive approach to analysing talk in strategy meetings', *British Journal of Management*, 23: 455–73.

Clegg, S., Kornberger, M., and Rhodes, C. (2007), 'Business ethics as practice', *British Journal of Management*, 18: 107–22.

Code of Conduct (2015). Retrieved 2015-11-10, from www.lofbergs.se/wp-content/uploads/2015/12/code-of-conduct-materials-equipments-and-services-eng.version-74.pdf

Coffee Group Document (2012–2016). Retrieved 2016-11-10, from https://en.lofbergs.se

Coffee Kids (2015). Retrieved 2016-11-23, from www.scaa.org/chronicle/2015/04/11/a-new-lease-on-life-for-coffee-kids

Cohen-Charash, Y., and Spector, P. E. (2001), 'The role of justice in organizations: A meta-analysis', *Organizational Behavior and Human Decision Processes*, 86/2: 278–321.

Coleman, J. S. (1990), *Foundations of Social Theory*. Cambridge, MA: Harvard University Press.

Colquitt, J. A., Conlon, D. E., Wesson, M. J., Porter, C. O. L. H., and Ng, K. Y. (2001), 'Justice at the Millennium: A meta-analytic review of 25 years of organizational justice research', *Journal of Applied Psychology*, 86/3: 425–45.

Connelly, B., Ketchen, D. J., and Slater, S. F. (2011), 'Toward a"theoretical toolbox" for sustainability research in marketing', *Journal of the Academy of Marketing Science*, 39/1:86–100.

Cooper, R. (2005), 'Peripheral vision: Relationality', *Organization Studies*, 26: 1689–1710.

Cooren, F., Bencherki, N., Chaput, M., and Vásquez, C. (2015), 'The communicative constitution of strategy-making: Exploring fleeting moments of strategy', in Golsorkhi, D., Rouleau, L., Seidl, D., and Vaara, E. (eds.), *Cambridge Handbook of Strategy as Practice*, 365–88. Cambridge: Cambridge University Press.

Cornelissen, J., and Schildt, H. (2015), 'Sensemaking in strategy as practice: As phenomenon or a perspective?', in Golsorkhi, D., Rouleau, L., Seidl, D., and Vaara, E. (eds.), *Cambridge Handbook of Strategy as Practice*, 345–64. Cambridge: Cambridge University Press.

Cornut, F., Giroux, H., and Langley, A. (2012), 'The strategic plan as a genre', *Discourse & Communication*, 6/1: 21–54.

Crain, W. (1992), *Theories of Development Concepts and Applications*. London: Prentice Hall.

CSR Europe, About Us (2015). Retrieved 2016-11-23, from www.csreurope .org/about-us

CSR Sweden (2015). Retrieved 2016-11-23, from https://sweden.se/business/ csr-in-sweden/

Cunliffe, A. L. (2015), 'Using ethnography in strategy-as-practice research', in Golsorkhi, D., Rouleau, L., Seidl, D., and Vaara, E. (eds.), *Cambridge Handbook of Strategy as Practice*, 431–46. Cambridge: Cambridge University Press.

(2002), 'Social poetics as management inquiry: A dialogical approach', *Journal of Management Inquiry*, 11: 128–45.

Czarniawska, B. (1997), *Narrating the Organization*, Chicago: The University of Chicago Press.

D'Adderio, L. (2008), 'The performativity of routines: Theorising the influence of artefacts and distributed agencies on routine dynamics', *Research Policy*, 37: 769–89.

Dameron, S., and Torset, C. (2014), 'The discursive construction of strategists' subjectivities: Towards a paradox lens on strategy', *Journal of Management Studies*, 51/2: 291–319.

Danley, J. R. (1980), 'Corporate moral agency: The case for anthropological bigotry', *Bowling Green Studies in Applied Philosophy*, 2: 140–49.

Dean, T., and McMullen, J. S. (2007), 'Toward a theory of sustainable entrepreneurship: Reducing environmental degradation through entrepreneurial actions', *Journal of Business Venturing*, 22/1: 50–76.

Definition Cover Crop Small Farms (2016). Retrieved 2016-11-17, from http://smallfarm.about.com/od/glossary/g/Cover-Crop.htm

DeGroat, C. (2016), *Wholeheartedness: Busyness, Exhaustion, and Healing the Divided Self*. Grand Rapids, Michigan: William, B. Eerdmans.

De La Ville, V-I., and Mounoud, E. (2015), 'A narrative approach to strategy as practice: Strategy-making from texts and narratives', in Golsorkhi, D., Rouleau, L., Seidl, D., and Vaara, E. (eds.), *Cambridge Handbook of Strategy as Practice*, 249–64. Cambridge: Cambridge University Press.

Delbridge, R., and Edwards, T. (2013), 'Inhabiting institutions: Critical realist refinements to understanding institutional complexity and change', *Organization Studies*, 34/7: 927–47.

Descartes, R. (1968), *Discourse on Method and the Meditations*. London: Penguin Books.

Dilthey, W. (1985), *Poetry and Experience*. Princeton, NJ: Princeton University Press.

Donaldson, T. (2003), 'Editor's comments: Taking ethics seriously – a mission now more possible', *The Academy of Management Review*, 28/3: 363–66.

Donaldson, T., and Dunfee, T. W. (1994), 'Toward a unified conception of business ethics: Integrative social contracts theory', *The Academy of Management Review*, 19/2: 252–84.

Donaldson, T., and Preston, L. E. (1995), 'The stakeholder theory of the corporation: Concepts, evidence, and implications', *The Academy of Management Review*, 20/1: 65–91.

Dreier, O. (2003), 'Re-searching psychotherapeutic practice', in Chaiklin, S., and Lave, J. (eds.), *Understanding Practice: Perspectives on Activity and Context*, 104–24. Cambridge: Cambridge University Press.

Edvardsson, B., Enquist, B., and Hay, M. (2006), 'Values based service brands: Narratives form IKEA', *Managing Service Quality*, 16/3: 230–46.

Elkington, J. (1998), 'Partnerships form cannibals with forks: The triple bottom line of 21st-century business', *Environmental Quality Management*, Autumn: 37–51.

Elms, H., Brammer, S., Harris, J. D., and Philips, R. A. (2010), 'New directions in strategic management and business ethics', *Business Ethics Quarterly*, 20/3: 401–25.

Emirbayer, M., and Mische, A. (1998), 'What is agency?', *The American Journal of Sociology*, 103/4: 962–1023.

Enquist, B-J. (2007), *Values drive value when crating sustainable service business. A study of a medium-sized values-driven company: Löfbergs Lila*. Master Thesis. Karlstad, Sweden: Karlstads University.

Enquist, B., Edvardsson, B., and Sebathu, P. (2008), 'Corporate social responsibility for charity or for service business?', *Asian Journal on Quality*, 9/1: 55–67.

Enquist, B., Johnsson, M., and Skålén, P. (2006), 'Adoption of corporate social responsibility – incorporating a stakeholder perspective', *Qualitative Research in Accounting & Management*, 3/3: 188–207.

Ericson, M. (2014), 'On the dynamics of fluidity and open-endedness of strategy process – toward a strategy-as-practicing conceptualization', *Scandinavian Journal of Management*, 30/1: 1–15.

(2010), *A Narrative Approach to Business Growth*. Cheltenham, UK, and Northampton, MA: Edward Elgar.

(2008), 'As in the Composition of a Fugue: Capturing the Flow of Strategic Business Activities', *International Journal of Qualitative Methods*, 7/2: 58–76.

(2007), *Business Growth – Activities, Themes and Voices*. Cheltenham, UK, and Northampton, MA: Edward Elgar.

(2004), *Strategic Change – Dualism, Duality, and Beyond*. Malmö/Copenhagen: Liber/Copenhagen Business School Press.

Ericson, M., Melin, L., and Popp, A. (2015), 'Studying strategy as practice through historical methods', in Golsorkhi, D., Rouleau, L., Seidl, D., and Vaara, E. (eds.), *Cambridge Handbook of Strategy as Practice*, 506–19. Cambridge: Cambridge University Press.

Etzioni, A. (1988), *The Moral Dimension: Toward a New Economics*. New York, NY: The Free Press.

European Commission Environment (2016), Retrieved 2016-11-17, from http://ec.europa.eu/environment/gpp/what_en.htm.

Evetts, J. (2003), 'The sociological analysis of professionalism', *International Sociology*, 18/2: 395–415.

Ezzamel, M., and Willmott, H. (2008), 'Strategy as discourse in a global retailer: A supplement to rationalist and interpretative accounts', *Organization Studies*, 29/2: 191–217.

Fair and Good (2013). Booklet. Karlstad, Sweden: AB Anders Löfberg.

Fairclough, N. (1989), *Language and Power*. London: Longman.

Fauré, B., and Rouleau, L. (2011), 'The strategic competence of accountants and middle managers in budget making', Accounting, *Organizations and Society*, 36/3: 167–82.

Fehr, E., and Gächter, S. (2000). 'Fairness and retaliation: The economics of reciprocity', *Journal of Economic Perspectives*, 14/3: 159–81.

Feldman, M. S. (2015), 'Theory of routine dynamics and connections to strategy as practice', in Golsorkhi, D., Rouleau, L., Seidl, D., and Vaara, E. (eds.), *Cambridge Handbook of Strategy as Practice*, 317–30. Cambridge: Cambridge University Press.

Feldman, M. S., and Pentland, B. T. (2003), 'Reconceptualizing organizational routines as a source of flexibility and change', *Administrative Science Quarterly*, 48: 94–118.

Fichtner, B. (1999), 'Activity revisited as an explanatory principle and as an object of study – old limits and new perspectives', in Chaiklin, S., Hedegaard, M., and Jensen, U. J.(eds.), *Activity Theory and Social Practice*, 51–65. Aarhus, Denmark: Aarhus University Press.

Fletcher, D. (2007), 'Toy story: The narrative world of entrepreneurship and the creation of interpretive communities', *Journal of Business Venturing*, 22: 649–72.

(2006), 'Entrepreneurial processes and the social construction of opportunity', *Entrepreneurship and Regional Development*, 18: 421–40.

(2003), 'Framing organizational emergence: Discourse, identity and relationship', in Steyaert, C., and Hjorth, D. (eds.), *New Movements in Entrepreneurship*, 125–42. Cheltenham, UK, and Northampton, MA: Edward Elgar.

Ford, R. C., and Richardson, W. D. (1994), 'Ethical decision making: A review of the empirical literature', *Journal of Business Ethics*, 13: 205–21.

Foucault, M. (2001), *Fearless Speech*. Los Angeles, CA: Semiotext(e).

(1980), *Power/Knowledge: Selected Interviews and Other Writings 1972–1977*. New York, NY: Pantheon Books.

(1972), *The Archeology of Knowledge*. London: Routledge

Franck, H. (2014), 'Paul Ricoeur (1913–2005)', in Helin, J., Hernes, T., Hjorth, D., and Holt, R. (eds.), *The Oxford Handbook of Process Philosophy and Organization Studies*, 454–64. Oxford: Oxford University Press.

Freeman, R. E. (2000), 'Business ethics at the millennium', *Business Ethics Quarterly*, 10/1: 169–80.

(1984), *Strategic Management: A Stakeholder Approach*. Boston: Pitman.

Freeman, R. E., Harrison, J. S., Wicks, A. C., Parmar, B. L., and de Colle, S. (2010), *Stakeholder Theory: The State of the Art*. Cambridge: Cambridge University Press.

Friedman, M. (1962), *Capitalism and Freedom*. Chicago: University of Chicago Press.

FTI (2015), Retrieved 2016-11-23, from www.ftiab.se/257.html

FTI's Instructions (2015). Retrieved 2016-11-23, from www.ftiab.se/download/ 18.199e376014de455633711b/1434550782449/Instructions+eng++2015-06-17.pdf

Gadamer, H-G. (1989), *Truth and Method*. New York, NY: The Continuum.

Gergen, K. J. (1999), *An Invitation to Social Construction*. Thousand Oaks, CA: Sage.

Get to Know a Good Coffee (2013), Booklet. Karlstad, Sweden: AB Anders Löfberg.

Ghoshal, S. (2005), 'Bad management theories are destroying good management practices', *Academy of Management Learning & Education*, 4/1: 75–91.

Gibson, K. (2007), *Ethics and Business: An Introduction*. Cambridge: Cambridge University Press.

Giddens, A. (1979), *Central Problems in Social Theory: Action, Structure and Contradiction in Social Analysis*. Berkeley/Los Angeles, CA: University of California Press.

Gintis, H., and Khurana, R. (2008), 'Corporate honesty and business education: A behavioral model', in Zak, P. J. (ed.), *Moral Markets: The Critical Role of Values in the Economy*, 300–27. Princeton, NJ: Princeton University Press.

Golsorkhi, D., Rouleau, L., Seidl, D., and Vaara, E. (eds.) (2015), *Cambridge Handbook of Strategy as Practice*. Cambridge: Cambridge University Press.

Gomez, M-L. (2015), 'A Bourdieusian perspective on strategizing', in Golsorkhi, D., Rouleau, L., Seidl, D., and Vaara, E. (eds.), *Cambridge Handbook of Strategy as Practice*, 184–98. Cambridge: Cambridge University Press.

Gomez, M-L., and Bouty, I. (2011), 'The emergence of an influential practice: Food for thought', *Organization Studies*, 32/7: 921–40.

Goodenough, O. R. (2008), 'Values, mechanism, design, and fairness', in Zak, P. J. (ed.), *Moral Markets. The Critical Role of Values in the Economy*, 228–55. Princeton, NJ: Princeton University Press.

Goodenough, O. R., and Gruter Cheney, M. (2008), 'Preface', in Zak, P. J. (ed.), *Moral Markets. The Critical Role of Values in the Economy*, xxiii–xxx. Princeton, NJ: Princeton University Press.

Good for Life Charity (2015). Retrieved 2016-11-23, from www.goodfor lifecharity.org.uk/economic-development-in-the-ixil-region

Goodpaster, K. E. (1991), 'Business ethics and stakeholder analysis', *Business Ethics Quarterly*, 1/1: 53–73.

Grand, S., von Arx, W., and Rüegg-Stürm, J. (2015), 'Constructivist paradigms: Implications for strategy-as-practice research', in Golsorkhi, D., Rouleau, L., Seidl, D., and Vaara, E. (eds.), *Cambridge Handbook of Strategy as Practice*, 78–94. Cambridge: Cambridge University Press.

Grant, B. L. (2015). 'What is gypsum: Using gypsum for garden tilth'. Retrieved 2016-11-17, from www.gardeningknowhow.com/garden-how-to/soil-fertilizers/using-gypsum-in-garden.htm

Grönroos, C. (2000), *Service Management and Marketing: A Customer Relationship Management Approach*. Chichester, UK: Wiley.

Gustafsson, C. (1994), 'Moralization as a link between idealism and naturalism in the ethical discourse', in De Geer, H. (ed.), *Business Ethics in Progress?*, 115–24. Berlin/New York, NY: Springer-Verlag.

(1991), *New Values, Morality and Strategic Ethics*. Memo-stencil, Nr 148. Åbo, Finland: Åbo Academi University.

Haag, K. (2012), *Rethinking Family Business Succession: From a Problem to Solve to an Ongoing Practice*. Doctoral dissertation. Jönköping, Sweden: Jönköping International Business School.

Hall, A. (2003), *Strategising in the Context of Genuine Relations: An Interpretative Study of Strategic Renewal through Family Interaction*. Doctoral dissertation. Jönköping, Sweden: Jönköping International Business School.

Hall, A., Melin, L., and Nordqvist, M. (2006), 'Understanding strategizing in the family business context, in Poutziouris, P. Z., Smyrnios, K. X., and Klein, S. B. (eds.), *Handbook of Research on Family Business*, 253–68. Cheltenham, UK, and Northampton, MA: Edward Elgar.

Hardy, C., and Thomas, R. (2014), 'Strategy, discourse and practice: The intensification of power', *Journal of Management Studies*, 51/2: 320–48.

Harrison, J. S., and Freeman, R. E. (1999), 'Stakeholders, social responsibility, and performance: Empirical evidence and theoretical perspectives', *Academy of Management Journal*, 42/5: 479–85.

Hartley, C. (2014), 'Two conceptions of justice as reciprocity', *Social Theory and Practice*, 40/3: 409–32.

Hartman, E. M. (2000), 'Socratic ethics and the challenge of globalization', *Business Ethics Quarterly*, 10/1: 211–20.

(2013), *Virtue in Business: Conversations with Aristotle*. Cambridge: Cambridge University Press

Helin, J. (2011), *Living Moments in Family Meetings: A Process Study in the Family Business Context.* Doctoral dissertation. Jönköping, Sweden: Jönköping International Business School.

Helin, J., Hernes, T., Hjorth, D., and Holt, R. (2014), 'Process is how process does', in Helin, J., Hernes, T., Hjorth, D., and Holt, R. (eds.), *The Oxford Handbook of Process Philosophy & Organization Studies*, 1–16. Oxford: Oxford University Press.

Hemphill, T. A. (2004), 'Corporate citizenship: The case for a new corporate governance model', *Business and Society Review*, 109/3: 339–61.

Herman, V. (1995), *Dramatic Discourse Dialogue as Interaction in Plays.* London: Routledge.

Hirsch Hadorn, G., Bradley, D., Pohl, C., Rist, S., and Wiesmann, U. (2006), 'Implications of transdisciplinarity for sustainability research', *Ecological Economics*, 60/1: 119–28.

Hirschman, A. O. (1970), *Exit, Voice, and Loyalty: Responses to Decline in Firms, Organizations, and States.* Cambridge, MA: Harvard University Press.

Hjorth, D., and Johannisson, B. (2007), 'Learning as an entrepreneurial process', in Fayolle, A. (ed.), *Handbook of Research in Entrepreneurship Education, Volume 1. A General Perspective*, 46–66. Cheltenham, UK, and Northampton, MA: Edward Elgar.

Hjorth, D., and Steyaert, C. (2004), *Narrative and Discursive Approaches in Entrepreneurship: A Second Movements in Entrepreneurship Book.* Cheltenham, UK, and Northampton, MA: Edward Elgar.

Hosmer, L. T. (1994), 'Strategic planning as if ethics mattered', *Strategic Management Journal*, 15: 17–34.

Husted, B. W., and Allen, D. B. (2010), *Corporate Social Strategy: Stakeholder Engagement and Competitive Advantage.* Cambridge: Cambridge University Press.

(2000), 'Is it ethical to use ethics as strategy?' *Business Ethics*, 27/1: 21–31.

Hutcheson, F. (2007), *Philosophae moralis insitutio compendiaria with a Short Introduction to Moral Philosophy.* Indianapolis: Liberty Fund.

Hållbar Livsmedelskedja (2016). Retrieved 2016-11-23, from http://hallbarlivsmedelskedja.se

Ibarra-Colado, E., Clegg, S. R., Rhodes, C., and Kornberger, M. (2006), 'The ethics of managerial subjectivity', *Journal of Business Ethics*, 64: 45–55.

International Coffee Partners, about Us (2016). Retrieved 2016-11-17, from www.coffee-partners.org/about-us

Jackson, W. A. (1999), 'Dualism, duality and the complexity of economic institutions', *International Journal of Social Economics*, 26/4: 545–58.

Jamali, D. (2008), 'A stakeholder approach to corporate social responsibility: A fresh perspective into theory and practice', *Journal of Business Ethics*, 82/1: 213–31.

Janney, J. J., and Folta, T. B., (2006), 'Moderating effects of investor experience on the signalling value of private equity placements', *Journal of Business Venturing*, 21: 27–44.

Jarzabkowski, P., and Spee, A. P. (2009), 'Strategy-as-practice: A review and future directions for the field', *International Journal of Management Reviews*, 11/1: 69–95.

Jarzabkowski, P., Balogun, J., and Seidl, D. (2007), 'Strategizing: The challenges of a practice perspective', *Human Relations*, 60/1: 5–27.

Jeanes, E. L., and Muhr, S. L. (2010), 'The impossibility of guidance – a Levinasian critique of business ethics', in Muhr, S. L., Sørensen, B. M., and Vallentin, S.(eds.), *Ethics and Organizational Practice – Questioning the Moral Foundation of Management*, 143–62. Cheltenham, UK, and Northampton, MA: Edward Elgar.

Jennings, B. (2010), 'Ethical aspects of sustainability', *Minding Nature*, 3/1: 1–2.

Jennings, D. P., and Zandbergen, P. A. (1995), 'Ecologically sustainable organizations: An institutional approach', *Academy of Management Review*, 20/4: 1015–52.

Joas, H. (1996), *The Creativity of Action*. Cambridge: Polity Press.

Johnson, G., Melin, L., and Whittington, R. (2003), 'Micro strategy and strategizing: Toward an activity-based view', *Journal of Management Studies*, 40/1: 3–22.

Johnson, G., Smith, S., and Codling, B. (2010), 'Institutional change and strategic agency: An empirical analysis of managers' experimentation with routines in strategic decision making', in Golsorkhi, D., Rouleau, L., Seidl, D., and Vaara, E. (eds.), *Cambridge Handbook of Strategy as Practice*, 273–90. Cambridge: Cambridge University Press.

Jonas, H. (1984), *The Imperative of Responsibility: In Search of an Ethics for the Technological Age*. Chicago: The University of Chicago Press.

Jones, T. M. (1995), 'Instrumental stakeholder theory: A synthesis of ethics and economics', *The Academy of Management Review*, 20/2: 404–37.

Jones, T. M., Felps, W., and Bigley, G. A. (2007), 'Ethical theory and stakeholder-related decisions: The role of stakeholder culture', *The Academy of Management Review*, 32/1: 137–55.

Jones, R., Latham, J., and Betta, M. (2008), 'Narrative construction of the social entrepreneurial identity', *International Journal of Entrepreneurial Behaviour & Research*, 14/5: 330–45.

Kafferosteriet Löfbergs (2016). Retrieved 2016-11-17, from www.lofbergs.se

Kang, Y. C., and Wood, D. J. (1995), 'Before-profit corporate social responsibility: Turning the economic paradigm upside-down', *Proceedings of the International Association for Business and Society*, 6: 809–29.

Kant, E. (1956), *Groundwork of the Metaphysic of Moral*. New York, NY: Harper & Row.

Kaplan, S. (2011), 'Strategy and power point: An inquiry into the epistemic culture and machinery of strategy making', *Organization Science*, 22/2: 320–46.

(2008), 'Framing contests: Strategy making under uncertainty', *Organization Science*, 19/5: 729–52.

Kaplan, S., and Orlikowski, W. J. (2013), 'Temporal work in strategy making', *Organization Science*, 24/4: 965–95.

Katz, J. S., and Martin, B. R. (1997), 'What is research collaboration?, *Research Policy*, 26/1: 1–18.

Keeley, M., and Graham, J. W. (1991), 'Exit, voice, and ethics', *Journal of Business Ethics*, 10: 349–55.

Klonoski, R. J. (1991), 'Foundational considerations in the corporate social responsibility debate', *Business Horizons*, 34/4: 9–18.

Knights, D. (1997),' Organization theory in the age of deconstruction: Dualism, gender and postmodernism revisited', *Organization Studies*, 18/1: 1–19.

Knights, D., and Morgan, G. (1991), 'Corporate strategy, organizations, and subjectivity: A critique', *Organization Studies*, 12/2: 251–73.

Kornberger, M., and Clegg, S. (2011), 'Strategy as performative practice: The case of Sydney 2030', *Strategic Organization*, 9/2: 36–62.

La Jevic, L., and Springgay, S. (2008), 'A/r/tography as an ethics of embodiment: Visual journal in preservice education', *Qualitative Inquiry*, 14/1: 67–89.

Laine, P-M., and Vaara, E. (2015), 'Participation in strategy work', in Golsorkhi, D., Rouleau, L., Seidl, D., and Vaara, E. (eds.), *Cambridge Handbook of Strategy as Practice*, 616–31. Cambridge: Cambridge University Press.

(2007), 'Struggling over subjectivity: A discursive analysis of strategic development in an engineering group', *Human Relations*, 60/1: 29–58.

Langley, A. (2015), 'The ongoing challenge of developing cumulative knowledge about strategy as practice', in Golsorkhi, D., Rouleau, L., Seidl, D., and Vaara, E. (eds.), *Cambridge Handbook of Strategy as Practice*, 111–27. Cambridge: Cambridge University Press.

Langley, A., and Lusiani, M. (2015), 'Strategic planning as practice', in Golsorkhi, D., Rouleau, L., Seidl, D., and Vaara, E. (eds.), *Cambridge Handbook of Strategy as Practice*, 547–63. Cambridge: Cambridge University Press.

Laursen, B., and Hartup, W. W. (2002), 'The origins of reciprocity and social exchange in friendship', *New Directions for Child and Adolescent Development*, 95: 27–40.

Lave, J. (2003), 'The practice of learning', in Chaiklin, S., and Lave, J. (eds.), *Understanding Practice. Perspectives on Activity and Context*, 3-32. Cambridge: Cambridge University Press.

Lee, M-D. L. (2007), 'A review of the theories of corporate social responsibility: Its evolutionary path and the road ahead', *International Journal of Management Reviews*, 10/1: 53–73.

Lê, J., and Spee, P. (2015), 'The role of materiality in the practice of strategy', in Golsorkhi, D., Rouleau, L., Seidl, D., and Vaara, E. (eds.), *Cambridge Handbook of Strategy as Practice*, 582–97. Cambridge: Cambridge University Press.

Leonardi, P. M. (2011), 'When flexible routines meet flexible technologies: Affordance, constraint, and the imbrications of human and material agencies', *MIS Quarterly*, 35/1: 147–67.

Levinas, E. (1991), *Otherwise Than Being or beyond Essence*. Dordrecht: Kluwer.

(1987), *Time and the Other*. Pittsburgh: Duquesne University Press.

Levitt, T. (1983), 'The dangers of social responsibility', in Beauchamp, T. L., and Bowie, N. E. (eds.), *Ethical Theory and Business*, 83–6. Englewood Cliffs, NJ: Prentice Hall.

Levy, D., Reinecke, J., and Manning, S. (2016), 'The political dynamics of sustainable coffee: Contested value regimes and the transformation of sustainability', *Journal of Management Studies*, 53/3: 364–97.

Lewis, A., and Wärneryd, K-E. (1994) (eds.), *Ethics and Economic Affairs*. London/New York, NY: Routledge.

Ling, Y., Simsek, Z., Lubatkin, M. H., and Veiga, J. F. (2008), 'Transformational leadership's role in promoting corporate entrepreneurship: Examining the CEO-TMT interface', *The Academy of Management Journal*, 51/3: 557–76.

Liu, F., and Maitlis, S. (2014), 'Emotional dynamics and strategizing processes: A study of strategic conversations in top management teams', *Journal of Management Studies*, 51/2: 202–34.

Loacker, B., and Muhr, S. L. (2009), 'How can I become a responsible subject? Towards a practice-based ethics of responsiveness', *Journal of Business Ethics*, 90/2: 265–77.

Locke, J. (2008), *An Essay concerning Human Understanding*. Oxford: Oxford University Press.

Logsdon, J. M., and Wood, D. J. (2005), 'Global business citizenship and voluntary codes of ethics conduct', *Journal of Business Ethics*, 59/1: 55–67.

Luco, A. (2014), 'The definition of morality: Threading the needle', *Social Theory and Practice*, 40/3: 361–87.

Löfbergs Lila AB Annual Report, 2006/2007–2013/2014. Karlstad, Sweden: AB Anders Löfberg.

MacMillan, I. C. (1986), 'To really learn about entrepreneurship, let's study habitual entrepreneurs', *Journal of Business Venturing*, 1/3: 241–3.

Maitlis, S., and Christianson, M. (2014), 'Sensemaking in organizations: Taking stock and moving forward', *The Academy of Management Annals*, 8/1: 57–125.

Mantere, S. (2015), 'A Wittgenstein perspective on strategizing', in Golsorkhi, D., Rouleau, L., Seidl, D., and Vaara, E. (eds.), *Cambridge Handbook of Strategy as Practice*, 220–33. Cambridge: Cambridge University Press.

McDermott, R. P. (2003), 'The acquisition of a child by learning disability', in Chaiklin, S., and Lave, J. (eds.), *Understanding Practice: Perspectives on Activity and Context*, 269–305. Cambridge: Cambridge University Press.

McPhee, W. (2014), 'A new sustainability model: Engaging in the entire firm', *Journal of Business Strategy*, 35/2: 4–12.

Mead, G. H. (1932), *The Philosophy of the Present*. New York, NY: Prometheus Books.

Menon, A., and Menon, A. (1997), 'Enviropreneurial marketing strategy: The emergence of corporate environmentalism as market strategy', *Journal of Marketing*, 61/1: 51–67.

Meyer, J. P., and Allen, N. J. (1991), 'A three-component conceptualization of organizational commitment', *Human Resource Management Review*, 1: 64–89.

Meyer, J. P., and Parfyonova, N. M. (2010), 'Normative commitment in the workplace: A theoretical analysis and re-conceptualization', *Human Resource Management Review*, 20: 283–94.

Mill, J. S. (1998), *Utiliarianism*. Oxford: Oxford University Press.

Mische, A. (2009), 'Projects and possibilities: Researching futures in action', *Sociological Forum*, 24/3: 604–704.

Mitchell, R. K., Agle, B. R., and Wood, D. J. (1997), 'Toward a theory of stakeholder identification and salience: Defining the principle of who and what really accounts', *The Academy of Management Review*, 22/4: 853–86.

Moon, J., and Vogel, D. (2013), 'Corporate social responsibility, corporate governance and corporate regulation', in Rahim, M. M. (ed.), *Legal Regulation of Corporate Social Responsibility: A Meta-Regulation Approach of Law for Raising in a Weak Economy (CSR, Sustainability, Ethics & Governance)*, 13–46. Berlin/Heidelberg: Springer-Verlag.

Mößner, A. K. (2014), *Corporate social responsibility in the coffee sector. Löfbergs' CSR work towards sustainable development in Brazil's coffee chain.* Master Thesis. Copenhagen, Denmark: Aalborg University.

Nancy, J. L. (2000), *Of Being Singular Plural*. Stanford, CA: Stanford University Press.

Neubauer, H. (2003). The dynamics of succession in family businesses in Western European countries. *Family Business Review*, 16: 269–81.

Nevins, J. L., Bearden, W. O., and Money, B. (2007), 'Ethical values and long-term orientation', *Journal of Business Ethics*, 71: 261–74.

Nohria, N. (2013), Managers have a large impact on the ethical or unethical conduct of their employees. Retrieved 2016-05-23, from http://theoathproject.org/?p=166

Nordqvist, M. (2011), 'Understanding strategy processes in family firms: Exploring the roles of actors and arenas', *International Small Business Journal*, 30/1: 24–40.

   (2005), *Understanding the Role of Ownership in Strategizing: A Study of Family Firms*. Doctoral dissertation. Jönköping, Sweden: Jönköping International Business School.

Nordqvist, M., and Melin, L. (2010), 'Entrepreneurial families and family firms', *Entrepreneurship & Regional Development*, 22/3–4: 211–39.

   (2008), 'Strategic planning champions: Social craftsperson, artful interpreters and known stranger', *Long Range Planning*, 41:326–44.

Nordqvist, M., Habbershon, T. G., and Melin, L. (2008), 'Transgenerational entrepreneurship: Exploring entrepreneurial orientation in family firms', in Landström, H., Crijns, H., Laveren, E., and Smallbone, D. (eds.), *Entrepreneurship, Sustainable Growth and Performance: Frontiers in European Entrepreneurship Research*, 93–116. Cheltenham, UK, and Northampton, MA: Edward Elgar.

Norman, W., and MacDonald, C. (2004), 'Getting to the bottom of triple bottom line', *Business Ethics Quarterly*, 14/2: 243–62.

Orlikowski, W. J. (1996), 'Improvising organizational transformation over time: A situated change perspective', *Information Systems Research*, 7/1: 63–92.

Orlikowski, W. J., and Scott, S. V. (2008), 'Sociomateriality: Challenging the separation of technology work and organization', *The Academy of Management Annals*, 2/1: 433–74.

Orsi, F. (2015), *Value Theory*. London: Bloomsbury.

Painter-Morland, M., and ten Bos, R. (2011), 'Introduction: Critical crosssings', in Painter-Morland, M., and ten Bos, R. (eds.), *Business Ethics and Continental Philosophy*, 1–14. Cambridge: Cambridge University Press.

Parson, T. (1968), *The Structure of Social Action*. New York, NY: Free Press.

Parthemore, J., and Whitby, B. (2013), 'What makes any agent a moral agent? Reflections of machine consciousness and moral agency', *International Journal of Machine Consciousness*, 5/2: 105–29.

Persson, L. (2008), *Ethics and environment in the coffee sector – linking CSR to the consumer's power in the context of sustainable development. A case study of Löfbergs Lila*. Master Thesis. Karlstad, Sweden: Karlstads University.

Pestoff, V. A. (1991), *Between Market and Politics: Co-operatives in Sweden*. Boulder, CO: Westview Press.

Pettigrew, A. M., Woodman, R. W., and Cameron, K. S. (2001), 'Studying organizational change and development: Challenges for future research', *The Academy of Management Journal*, 44/4: 697–713.

Philips, N., and Oswick, C. (2012), 'Organizational discourse: Domains, debates, and directions', *The Academy of Management Annals'*, 6/1: 435–81.

Plato (2000), *The Republic*. Cambridge: Cambridge University Press.

Plessner Lyons, N. (1983), 'Two perspectives: On self, relationships, and morality', *Harvard Educational Review*, 53/2: 125–37.

Polkinghorne, D. E. (1988), *Narrative Knowing and the Human Sciences*. New York, NY: State University of New York Press.

Porter, M. E., and Kramer, M. R. (2006), 'Strategy & society: The link between competitive advantaged and corporate social responsibility', *Harvard Business Review*, 84/12: 78–90.

Press release, August 31, 2016. Retrieved 2016-11-23, from www.mynewsdesk .com/lofbergs/pressreleases/loefbergs-anna-nordstroem-is-swedens-first-sensory-professional-in-coffee-1539867

Press release database, European Commission (2016). Retrieved 2016-02-27 from http://europa.eu/rapid/press-release_MEMO-11–730_en.htm

Projects Brazil (2015). Retrieved 2016-11-17, from www.coffee-partners.org/ projects/region/brazil/project/farmer-story-meet-sr-jesus-lourenco-da-silva

Projects Tanzania, International Coffee Partners (2016). Retrieved 2016-11-17, from www.coffee-partners.org/projects/region/brazil/project/farmer-story-meet-sr-jesus-lourenco-da-silva

Pälli, P., Vaara, E., and Sorsa, V. (2009), 'Strategy as text and discursive practice: A genre-base approach in City administration', *Discourse & Communication*, 3/3: 309–18.

Raffnsøe, Møl Dalsgaard and Gudmand-Höyer (2014), 'Søren Kierkegaard (1813–1855)', in Helin, J., Hernes, T., Hjorth, D., and Holt, R. (eds.), *The*

Oxford Handbook of Process Philosophy and Organization Studies, 111–28. Oxford: Oxford University Press.

Rawls, J. (2000), *Lectures on the History of Moral Philosophy*. Cambridge, MA: Harvard University Press.

(1971), *A Theory of Justice*. Cambridge, MA: Harvard University Press.

Regnér, P. (2015), 'Relating strategy as practice to the resource-based view, capabilities perspectives and the micro-foundations approach', in Golsorkhi, D., Rouleau, L., Seidl, D., and Vaara, E. (eds.), *Cambridge Handbook of Strategy as Practice*, 301–16. Cambridge: Cambridge University Press.

(2008), 'Strategy-as-practice and dynamic capabilities: Steps towards a dynamic view of strategy', *Human Relations*, 61/4: 565–88.

Rescher, N. (2009), *Free Will: A Philosophical Reappraisal*. New Brunswick, NJ: Transaction.

Rhodes, C. (2011), 'Organizational justice', in Painter-Morland, M., and ten Bos, R. (eds.), *Business Ethics and Continental Philosophy*, 141–61. Cambridge: Cambridge University Press.

Rhodes, C., Pullen, A., and Clegg, S. R. (2010), '"If I should fall from grace ...": Stories of change and organizational ethics', *Journal of Business Ethics*, 91: 535–51.

Ricoeur, P. (2007), *Reflections of the Just*. Chicago: The University of Chicago Press.

(1992), *Oneself as the Other*. Chicago: The University of Chicago Press.

(1991), *From Text to Action: Essays in Hermeneutics, II*. Evanston, IL: Northwestern University Press.

(1984), *Time and Narrative*, vol. 3. Chicago: The University of Chicago Press.

Risser, J. (1981), *Hermeneutics and the Voice of the Other: Re-Reading Gadamer' Philosopical Hermeneutics*. New York, NY: State University of New York Press.

Rockström, J. (2009), 'A safe operating space for humanity', *Feature*, 461: 472–75.

Romero, K. C., and Lamadrid, R. L. (2014), 'Rethinking corporate social responsibility within the sustainability agenda. Issues and challenges for Asian-based companies', *Journal of Global Responsibility*, 5/2: 180–202.

Rouleau, L. (2015), 'Studying strategizing through biographical methods: Narratives of practices and life trajectories of practitioners', in Golsorkhi, D., Rouleau, L., Seidl, D., and Vaara, E. (eds.), *Cambridge Handbook of Strategy as Practice*, 462–76. Cambridge: Cambridge University Press.

(2005), 'Micro-practices of strategic sensemaking and sensegiving: How middle managers interpret and sell change every day', *Journal of Management Studies*, 42/7: 1413–41.

Rouleau, L., and Balogun, J. (2011), 'Middle managers, strategic sensemaking, and discursive competence', *Journal of Management Studies*, 48/5: 953–83.

Rouleau, L., Balogun, J., and Floyd, S. W. (2015), 'Strategy-a-practice research on middle managers' strategy work', in Golsorkhi, D., Rouleau, L., Seidl, D., and Vaara, E. (eds.), *Cambridge Handbook of Strategy as Practice*, 598–615. Cambridge: Cambridge University Press.

Rousseau, J-J. (2003), *ÉMILE or Treatise on Education*. New York, NY: Prometheus Books.

Sachs, S., and Rühli, E. (2011), *Stakeholders Matter: A New Paradigm for Strategy in Society*. Cambridge: Cambridge University Press.

Salvato, C. (2003), 'The role of micro-strategies in the engineering of firm evolution', *Journal of Management Studies*, 40/1: 83–108.

Salvato, C., and Rerup, C. (2011), 'Beyond collective entities: Multilevel research on organizational routines and capabilities', *Journal of Management*, 37/2: 468–90.

Samra-Fredericks, D. (2015), 'Researching everyday practice: The ethnomethodological contribution', in Golsorkhi, D., Rouleau, L., Seidl, D., and Vaara, E. (eds.), *Cambridge Handbook of Strategy as Practice*, 477–90. Cambridge: Cambridge University Press.

(2003), 'Strategizing as lived experience and practitioners' everyday efforts to shape strategic direction', *Journal of Management Studies*, 40/1: 141–74.

Sandberg, J., and Dall'Alba, G. (2009), 'Returning to practice anew: A life-world perspective', *Organization Studies*, 30/12: 1349–68.

Sandberg, J., and Tsoukas, H. (2011), 'Grasping the logic of practice: Theorizing through practical rationality', *Academy of Management Review*, 36/2: 338–60.

Schatzki, T. R. (1996), *Social Practices: A Wittgenstein Approach to Human Activity and the Social*. New York, NY: Cambridge University Press.

Schendel, D., and Hofer, C. W. (1979), *Strategic Management: A New View of Business Policy and Planning*. Boston: Little, Brown.

Schutz, A. (1967), *The Phenomenology of the Social World*. Evanston, IL: Northwestern University Press.

Schultze, W. S., Lubatkin, M. H., and Dino, R. N. (2003), 'Exploring the agency consequences of ownership among directors of private family firms', *The Academy of Management Journal*, 46/2: 179–94.

Schwartz, M. S. (2005), 'Universal moral values for corporate codes of ethics', *Journal of Business Ethics*, 59: 27–44.

Seidl, D., and Guérard, S. (2015), 'Meetings and workshops as strategy practices', in Golsorkhi, D., Rouleau, L., Seidl, D., and Vaara, E. (eds.), *Cambridge Handbook of Strategy as Practice*, 564–81. Cambridge: Cambridge University Press.

Shafer-Landau, R. (2012), *The Fundamentals of Ethics*. Oxford/New York, NY: Oxford University Press.

Sharma, P. (2006), 'An overview of the field of family business studies: Current status and directions for the future', in Poutziouris, P. Z., Smyrnios, K. X., and Klein, S. B. (eds.), *Handbook of Research on Family Business*, 253–68. Cheltenham, UK, and Northampton, MA: Edward Elgar.

Shepherd, D., and Haynie, M. J. (2009), 'Family business, identity conflict, and an expedited entrepreneurial process: A process of resolving identity conflict', *Entrepreneurship Theory & Practice*, 33/6: 1245–64.

Shotter, J. (2006), 'Understanding process from within: An argument for "withness"-thinking', *Organization Studies*, 27/4: 585–604.

Shrivastava, P. (1995), 'Environmental technologies and competitive advantages', *Strategic Management Journal*, 16/1: 183–200.

SIDA (2015). Retrieved 2016-11-23, from www.sida.se/Svenska/sa-arbetar-vi/
Detta-ar-svenskt-bistand/Sveriges-bistandslander

Sillince, J., Jarzabkowski, P., and Shaw, D. (2012), 'Shaping strategic action
through the rhetorical construction and exploitation of ambiguity',
Organization Science, 23/3: 630–50.

Simon, H. (1947), *Administrative Behavior: A Study of Decision-Making Processes
in Administrative Organization*. London: The Free Press.

Singer, A. E. (1994), 'Strategy as moral philosophy', *Strategic Management
Journal*, 15: 191–213.

Sinnott, K. (2010), *The Art and Craft of Coffee: An Enthusiasts' Guide to Selecting,
Roasting, and Brewing Exquisite Coffee*. Beverly, MA: Quarry Books.

Sison, A. J. G. (2014), *Happiness and Virtue Ethics in Business: The Ultimate Value
Proposition*. Cambridge: Cambridge University Press.

Skitka, L. J., Bauman, C. W., and Mullen, E. (2008), 'Morality and justice: An
expanded theoretical perspective and empirical review', in Hedgvedt, K. A.,
and Clay-Werner, J. (eds.), Advances in Group Processes, *vol. 25*:1–27.
Bingley, UK: Emerald Group.

Smith. A. (1976), *The Theory of Moral Sentiments*. Oxford: Oxford University
Press.

Solomon, R. C. (2008), 'Free enterprise, sympathy, and virtue', in Zak, P. J.
(ed.), *Moral Markets: The Critical Role of Values in the Economy*, 16–41.
Princeton, NJ: Princeton University Press.

Somers, M. R. (1994), 'The narrative of identity: A relations and network
approach', *Theory and Society*, 23: 605–49.

Spee, P. A., and Jarzabkowski, P. (2011), 'Strategic planning as communicative
process', *Organization Studies*, 32/9: 1217–45.

Splitter, V., and Seidl, D. (2015), 'Practical relevance of practice-based research
on strategy', in Golsorkhi, D., Rouleau, L., Seidl, D., and Vaara, E. (eds.),
Cambridge Handbook of Strategy as Practice, 128–41. Cambridge: Cambridge
University Press.

 (2011), 'Does practice-based research on strategy lead to practically relevant
knowledge? Implications of a Bourdieusian perspective', *Journal of Applied
Behavioral Science*, 47/1: 98–120.

Stanford Encyclopedia of Philosophy (2016). Retrieved 2016-03-29, from http://
plato.stanford.edu/entries/stoicism

Starkey, K., and Crane, A. (2003), 'Towards green narrative: Management and
the evolutionary epic', *Academy of Management Review'*, 28/2: 220–37.

Stefanovic, I. L. (2000), 'Phenomenological reflections on ecosystem health',
Ethics and the Environment, 5/2: 253–69.

Stensaker, L., and Falkenberg, J. (2007), 'Making sense of different responses to
corporate change', *Human Relations*, 60/1: 137–77.

Steyaert, C. (2007), 'Entrepreneuring' as a conceptual attractor? A review of
process theories in 20 years of entrepreneurship studies', *Entrepreneurship
and Regional Development*, 19: 453–77.

Stone, P. J. (1994), 'Exit or voice? Lessons from companies in South Africa', in
Lewis, A., and Wärneryd, K-E. (1994) (eds.), *Ethics and Economic Affairs*,
17–38. London/New York, NY: Routledge.

Stout, L. A. (2008), 'Taking conscience seriously', in Zak, P. J. (ed.), *Moral Markets: The Critical Role of Values in the Economy*, 157–72. Princeton, NJ: Princeton University Press.

Suchman, L. A., and R. H. Trigg (2003), 'Artificial intelligence as craftwork', in Chaiklin, S., and Lave, J. (eds.), *Understanding Practice: Perspectives on Activity and Context*, 144–78. Cambridge: Cambridge University Press.

Sustainability Report2012/2013. Karlstad, Sweden: AB Anders Löfberg.

Svensson, G., and Wood, G. (2008), 'A model of business ethics', *Journal of Business Ethics*, 77/3: 303–22.

Swedish Leadership for Sustainable Development (2015). Retrieved 2016-11-23, from www.sida.se/English/how-we-work/approaches-and-methods/ funding/financing-for-development/swedish-leadership-for-sustainable-development

Taylor, C. (1989), *Sources of the Self: The Making of the Modern Identity*. Cambridge, MA: Harvard University Press.

ten Bos, R., and Dunne, S. (2011), 'Corporate social responsibility', in Painter-Morland, M., and ten Bos, R. (eds.), *Business Ethics and Continental Philosophy*, 242–62. Cambridge: Cambridge University Press.

The Haga Initiative (2015). Retrieved 2016-11-23, from http://hagainitiativet.se/ en/category/current

Todd, S. (2003), *Levinas, Psychoanalysis, and Ethical Possibilities in Education. Learning from the Other*. New York, NY: State University of New York Press.

Tsoukas, H. (2015), 'Making strategy: Meta-theoretical insights from Heideggerian phenomenology', in Golsorkhi, D., Rouleau, L., Seidl, D., and Vaara, E. (eds.), *Cambridge Handbook of Strategy as Practice*, 58–77. Cambridge: Cambridge University Press.

Tsoukas, H., and Chia, R. (2002), 'On organizational becoming: Rethinking organizational change', *Organization Science*, 13: 567–82.

UNICEF Annual Report (2015). Retrieved 2016-11-23, from www.unicef.org/ publications/index_92018.html

Vaara, E. (2015), 'Critical discourse analysis as methodology in strategy-as-practice research', in Golsorkhi, D., Rouleau, L., Seidl, D., and Vaara, E. (eds.), *Cambridge Handbook of Strategy as Practice*, 491–505. Cambridge: Cambridge University Press.

  (2010), 'Taking the linguistic turn seriously: Strategy as a multifaceted and interdiscursive phenomenon', *Advances in Strategic Management*, 27: 29–50.

Vaara, E., and Whittington, R. (2012), 'Strategy-as-practice: Taking social practices seriously', *The Academy of Management Annals*, 6/1: 285–336.

Vaara, E., Sorsa, V., and Pälli, P. (2010), 'On the force potential of strategy texts: A critical discourse analysis of a strategic plan and its power effects in a city organization', *Organization*, 17/6: 685–702.

Van Horn, G. (2015), Ethics and Sustainability: A Primer with Suggested Readings. Center for Humans & Nature. Retrieved 2015-10-18, from https://iseethics.files.wordpress.com/2013/09/ethics_and_sustainability_ primer.pdf

Van Manen, M. (1990), *Researching Lived Experience: Human Science for an Action Sensitive Pedagogy*. New York, NY: State University of New York Press.

Velázquez, A., Durán, E., Ramirez, I., Mas, J-F., Bocco, G., Ramirez, G., and Palacio, J-L. (2003), 'Land use-cover change processes in highly biodiverse areas: The case of Oaxaca, Mexico', *Global Environmental Change*, 13: 175–84.

Verbeke, A., and Tung, V. (2013), 'The future of stakeholder management theory: A temporal perspective', *Journal of Business Ethics*, 112/3: 529–43.

Vitell, S. J., and Hidalgo, E. R. (2006), 'The impact of corporate ethical of values and enforcement of ethical codes on the perceived importance of ethics in business: A comparison of U.S. and Spanish managers', *Journal of Business Ethics*, 64: 31–43.

Waddock, S. A., and Graves, S. B. (1997), 'The corporate social performance-financial performance link', *Strategic Management Journal*, 18/4: 303–19.

Waddock, S. A., and Leigh, J. (2006), 'The emergence of total responsibility management systems: J. Sainsbury's voluntary responsibility management system for global food retail supply chains', *Business and Society Review*, 111/4: 409–26.

Wartick, S. L., and Cochran, P. L. (1985), 'The evolution of the corporate performance model', *The Academy of Management Review*, 10/4: 758–69.

Watson, T. J. (2006), *Organising and Managing Work: Organisational, Managerial and Strategic Behavior in Theory and Practice*. Harlow, UK: Pearson.

We Work for the Coffee Growers for the Environment (2014). Booklet. Karlstad, Sweden: AB Anders Löfberg.

Webley, S., and Werner, A. (2008), 'Corporate codes of ethics: Necessary but not sufficient', *Business Ethics: A European Review*, 17/4: 406–15.

Weick, K. E. (1995), *Sensemaking in Organizations*. Thousand Oaks, CA: Sage.
(1979), *The Social Psychology of Organizing*. Reading, MA: Addison-Wesley.

Weik, E. (2014), 'Gottfried Leibniz (1646–1716)', in Helin, J., Hernes, T., Hjorth, D., and Holt, R. (eds.), *The Oxford Handbook of Process Philosophy and Organization Studies*, 94–110. Oxford: Oxford University Press.

Weiskopf, R., and Wilmott, H. (2013), 'Ethics as critical practice: The "Pentagon Papers", deciding responsibility, truth-telling, and the unsettling of organizational morality', *Organization Studies*, 34/4: 469–93.

Wells, G.A. (1993), *What's in a Name?* Chicago: Open Court.

Whittington, R. (2015), 'Giddens, structuration theory and strategy as practice', in Golsorkhi, D., Rouleau, L., Seidl, D., and Vaara, E. (eds.), *Cambridge Handbook of Strategy as Practice*, 145–64. Cambridge: Cambridge University Press.
(2006), 'Completing the practice turn in strategy research', *Organization Studies*, 27/5: 613–34.

Whittington, R., Jarzabkowski, P., Mayer, M., Mounoud, E., Nahapiet, J., and Rouleau, L. (2003), 'Taking strategy seriously: Responsibility and reform for an important social practice', *Journal of Management Inquiry*, 12/4: 396–409.

Wild, A. (2004), *Coffee: A Dark History*. New York/London: W. W. Norton.

Willmott, H. (2011). 'Enron narrative', in Painter-Morland, M., and ten Bos, R. (eds.), *Business Ethics and Continental Philosophy*, 96–116. Cambridge: Cambridge University Press.

Wittgenstein, L. (1953), *Philosophical Investigations*. Oxford, UK: Basil Blackwell.

Wood, D. J. (2010), 'Measuring corporate social performance: A review', *International Journal of Management Reviews*, 12/1: 50–84.

(1991), 'Corporate social performance revisited', *The Academy of Management Review*, 16/4: 691–718.

Zak, P. J. (2008), 'Introduction', in Zak, P. J. (ed.), *Moral Markets. The Critical Role of Values in the Economy*, xi–xxii. Princeton, NJ: Princeton University Press.

Zellweger, T. M., and Astrachan, J. H. (2008), 'On the emotional value of owning a firm', *Family Business Review*, 21/4: 347–63.

Index